GENOCIDE

The Systematic Killing of a People

Linda Jacobs Altman

—Issues in Focus—

ENSLOW PUBLISHERS,INC.

44 Fadem Road   P.O. Box 38
Box 699   Aldershot
Springfield, N.J. 07081   Hants GU12 6BP
U.S.A.   U.K.

Library of Congress Cataloging-in-Publication Data

Altman, Linda Jacobs, 1943–
    Genocide: the systematic killing of a people / Linda Jacobs Altman.
        p. cm. — (Issues in focus)
    Includes bibliographical references (p.) and index.
    ISBN 0-89490-664-X
    1. Genocide—History—Juvenile literature. [1. Genocide—History.] I. Title. II. Series:
Issues in focus (Springfield, N.J.)
D24.A57 1995
364.15'1'09—dc20   95-6941
                                              CIP
                                              AC

Printed in the United States of America

10 9 8 7 6 5 4 3 2 1

Illustration Credits: Arnold Kramer/United States Holocaust Memorial Museum,
p. 98; National Archives, pp. 12, 38, 51, 54, 58, 60, 65, 68, 72, 93, 95; Phoebe A.
Hearst Museum of Anthropology, The University of California at Berkeley, pp. 21,
29; United States Army Military History Institute, pp. 32, 82; United States
Holocaust Memorial Museum, pp. 7, 9, 70.

Cover Illustration: The dedication ceremony for the United States Holocaust
Memorial Museum, April 22, 1993. (Courtesy United States Holocaust Memorial
Museum)

Contents

1

The Night of Broken Glass

Germany. November 9, 1938. It was a tense Wednesday evening in Adolf Hitler's Third Reich: a seventeen-year-old Jewish student had assassinated a member of the German embassy staff. The Nazis immediately denounced the killing as part of a worldwide Jewish conspiracy against the German people.

Jews had been hounded, persecuted, and beaten in the streets ever since Hitler rose to power in 1933. Now the action of one Jew had given Propaganda Minister Joseph Goebbels an excuse to call for "spontaneous demonstrations" against all Jews.

Reinhard Heydrich, a brutal young officer of the SS (*Schutzstaffel*—"protection forces"), was responsible for organizing these demonstrations. At 1:20 A.M. on November 10, he teletyped orders to Nazi regional chiefs all over Germany, calling for the mass arrests of Jews and the destruction of their property.

In every city and town, brown-shirted Nazi storm troopers raged through Jewish neighborhoods, smashing windows, breaking doors, and forcing their way into Jewish homes. Unruly mobs of civilians joined in the carnage as Jews were chased, tormented, beaten—even killed.

An American eyewitness described the scene in the city of Leipzig on the night of November 9:

> Jewish dwellings were smashed into and the contents demolished or looted. In one of the Jewish sections, an eighteen-year-old boy was hurled from a three-story window to land with both legs broken on a street littered with burning beds and other household furniture. . . . Jewish shop windows by the hundreds were systematically and wantonly smashed throughout the city. . . . The main streets of the city were a positive litter of shattered plate glass.[1]

On the morning of November 10, just after Regina Auerbacher's father left the house to attend morning prayers at the synagogue, stones came hurling through every window in the house. "Soon we did not have a window in the house anymore," Auerbacher told *Newsweek* magazine. "All your life you relied on law and order. This time it was the government position to have no law and order."[2] Gangs broke windows and looted Jewish-owned businesses, while police rounded up Jewish men and took them to the city hall. From there, they were taken to the infamous Dachau concentration camp.

In Mannheim, nineteen-year-old Lotte Marshall awoke on Thursday morning to face unimaginable destruction: "The Torah scrolls, the prayer books and shawls were thrown in the

The Fasanenstrasse synagogue was one of 119 destroyed on Kristallnacht—the "Night of Broken Glass." For Germany's Jews, the tragedy and the terror of November 9 and 10, 1938, would soon be overshadowed by even greater horrors.

streets. We had a big beautiful synagogue. Now only pieces were standing."[3]

The architect of this horror, Reinhard Heydrich, pointed with pride to preliminary estimates of damage:

> The extent of the destruction of Jewish shops and houses cannot yet be verified . . . 815 shops destroyed, 171 dwelling houses set on fire or destroyed only indicate a fraction of the actual damage as far as arson is concerned . . . 119 synagogues were set on fire, and another 76 completely destroyed . . . 20,000 Jews were arrested. Thirty-six deaths were reported and those seriously injured were also numbered at thirty-six. Those killed and injured are Jews. . . .[4]

Later figures indicated that ninety-one Jews were killed and more than thirty thousand arrested. Nearly seventy-five hundred businesses and uncounted thousands of Jewish homes were totally destroyed. Before the rioting ended, whole neighborhoods and business districts lay in smoldering ruins. Shattered window glass lay in great piles on the sidewalks, hence the name *Kristallnacht* (the Night of Broken Glass). The cost in glass alone came to 5 million marks ($1.25 million in today's dollars). On November 12, Field Marshal Hermann Goering, who later would become Hitler's second in command, presided over a meeting of cabinet ministers and other high officials. Carefully and dispassionately, these men evaluated the results of Kristallnacht and discussed further steps against the Jews.

Goering decided to confiscate all insurance settlements payable to individual Jews for the damages of Kristallnacht and impose an additional fine of one billion marks upon the entire Jewish community "as punishment for their abominable

While the synagogue at Ober-Ramstad burns, a hose brigade prevents the fire from spreading to a nearby home. By order of the man who organized the "spontaneous demonstrations" of Kristallnacht, brigade members do nothing to stop the synagogue fire.

crimes." At the meeting, according to journalist and historian William Shirer:

> . . . it was agreed to solve the Jewish question in the following manner: eliminate the Jews from the German economy; transfer all Jewish business enterprises and property . . . to Aryan [German] hands with some compensation in bonds from which the Jews could use the interest but not the capital. The matter of excluding Jews from schools, resorts, parks, forests, etc., and of either expelling them after they had been deprived of all their property or confining them to German ghettos where they would be impressed as forced labor, was left for further consideration by a committee.[5]

So the horror began. Before it ended, six million Jews would perish in such death factories as Auschwitz, Sobibor, Majdanek, and Treblinka. The word *holocaust*, which literally means "total consumption by fire," would acquire a new and sinister meaning—the wholesale destruction of Jews by Nazi Germany.

2

Genocide: A History of Atrocity

During the period 1933 to 1945, before and during World War II, a small group of extremists planned and led the most systematic genocide in history. Though Nazi leaders issued the orders, they could not have killed those millions by themselves. Murder on a grand scale required the collaboration of ordinary, hardworking citizens who loved their families, gave to their local charities, and wouldn't think of mistreating their dogs.

In his study of the Holocaust, historian Martin Gilbert described the process that began with Hitler's rise to power in 1933 and continued until it had brutalized the whole of society: "The Germans who carried out the atrocities and cruelties had already become corrupted by their tasks; laughing when inflicting pain, and drawing in passers-by to laugh with them.

11

After the liberation of a concentration camp, former inmates pointed out guards and other camp officials who had been especially brutal. This Russian slave laborer accuses a former barracks guard.

Gradually entire populations became immune to feelings of outrage, and learned to shun compassion."[1]

Defining the Unthinkable

Before the Holocaust, there was no word to describe this process that turned one group of people into killers and another group into victims. In 1944, Ralph Lemkin, a Polish Jew who was a respected legal scholar, combined the Greek *genos* ("race" or "tribe") and the Latin *cide* ("killing") to form the word *genocide*. The United Nations Convention on Genocide broadened Lemkin's definition when it met in 1948. World War II was over by then, but a shaken world was still trying to come to terms with the Holocaust that had killed six million Jews and wiped out what was once a thriving Jewish community in Germany and Eastern Europe. With that horror still fresh in their minds, Convention members labored to define the unthinkable:

> In the present Convention, genocide means any of the following acts committed with intent to destroy, in whole or in part, a national, ethnic, racial, or religious group, as such:
>
> (a) Killing members of the group.
>
> (b) Causing serious bodily or mental harm to members of the group.
>
> (c) Deliberately inflicting on the group conditions of life calculated to bring about its physical destruction in whole or in part.
>
> (d) Imposing measures intended to prevent births within the group.
>
> (e) Forcibly transferring children of the group to another group.[2]

Others have found that definition too restrictive. Frank Chalk and Kurt Jonassohn of the Montreal Institute of Genocide Studies used the following: "Genocide is a form of one-sided mass killing in which a state or other authority intends to destroy a group, as that group and membership in it are defined by the perpetrator."[3]

This retains the United Nations emphasis on intent, while broadening the identification of victim groups: "While the United Nations definition is limited to national, ethnic, racial, or religious groups," wrote Jonassohn, "Chalk and I have argued that whatever group is being victimized is a 'group' in this context because the perpetrator has so defined it—even if no such 'group' exists outside the . . . vision of the perpetrator."[4]

Because both definitions consider intent as important as action, distinguishing systematic genocide from massacres, acts of war, and random human rights violations is not an easy task. For decades, sociologists have struggled to develop criteria for identifying past genocides and predicting future ones.

"Until we can predict when and where a genocide will occur, we cannot set up an early warning system," wrote Jonassohn. "But we certainly can recognize a genocide once it has started. . . . Mass killing does not ever occur without some preliminaries that can be used to recognize when the process of genocide is unfolding."[5]

The early stages of genocide may include official statements about "ethnic cleansing" or about "eliminating" a particular group, along with propaganda that portrays its members as evil or subhuman. This systematic dehumanization may be followed by massacres, mass arrests, forced marches, or deportations to slave labor camps.

14

According to Jonassohn, the appearance of refugees "is the best indicator" of the beginning of a genocide "because people do not leave their homes without their possessions, their families, and their friends unless they have genuine reasons to fear for their survival."[6]

Heretics, Infidels, and Holy Wars

The word *genocide* is modern, but the actions it describes are not new; human history is filled with systematic slaughters that would be called genocide by today's standards. The Assyrians under King Ashurnasirpal II (884–860 B.C.) used mass murder as a basic tactic of battle. After conquering a town, Ashurnasirpal's soldiers rounded up the inhabitants, cut off their hands and feet, and piled them in the town square to die. The only way a city could escape such a fate was to open its gates and surrender without a fight. If this happened, the king would settle for burning the town, torturing the mayor to death, and cutting off the legs of all military officers. He "generously" allowed everyone else to live, though of course they were taken from their homes and sold into slavery. Either way, an entire culture was destroyed.

In the Crusades of the Middle Ages, the destruction of entire populations took on a distinctly religious cast. Pope Urban II proclaimed the First Crusade in 1095, calling upon pious Christians to rescue the holy land of Palestine from those he called the infidel—non-Christian—Arabs. Hundreds of knights responded, taking solemn vows to commit their lives and property to the destruction of Muslims, Jews, and other non-Christians living in Palestine. In the name of God and of Truth, the crusaders slaughtered thousands, never questioning the morality of their acts or the superiority of their particular religious views.

A knight's account of the sack of Jerusalem describes the extent of the killing:

> Entering the city [July 15, 1099], our pilgrims pursued and killed Saracens [Muslims] up to the Temple of Solomon, in which they had assembled and where they gave battle to us furiously for the whole day so that their blood flowed through the whole temple. Finally, having overcome the pagans, our knights seized a great number of men and women, and they killed whom they wished and whom they wished they let live. . . . No one has even heard of or seen such a slaughter of pagan peoples since pyres were made of them like boundary marks, and no one except God knows their number.[7]

In the late twelfth and early thirteenth centuries, the Roman Catholic church began to mount crusades in Europe against those it considered heretics (Christians who held beliefs that contradicted established church doctrine). The most famous of these European crusades resulted in the destruction of the Albigensian sect in southern France. At one point, the Albigensians, or Cathari ("pure ones" or "saints") as they were sometimes called, were powerful enough to challenge the authority of the Roman Catholic church. The crusade wiped them out so thoroughly that almost all we know about Cathari beliefs and practices comes from the descriptions left by their enemies.

The church justified this slaughter by sounding what was to become a familiar theme in the annals of genocide: the enemy as a deadly infection. "In the eyes of the papacy and other orthodox believers," according to historian Norman F. Cantor, "the Albigensian domination of southern France constituted a cancer in the body of European civilization which had to be rooted out at all costs."[8]

The Inquisition

The theme that had justified the Crusades in the name of "true religion" sounded again in the late fifteenth century with the beginning of the Spanish Inquisition. Spain had been one of the most tolerant of European countries, with Christians, Muslims, and Jews living peaceably with one another and with Christian converts called Moriscos (former Muslims) and Marranos (former Jews).

Under the direction of Grand Inquisitor Tomás de Torquemada, that tolerance for diversity came to a bloody end. In the name of "the one true faith," Torquemada tortured prisoners until they confessed to heresy or witchcraft or some other dark crime. The confessed criminals were then burned at the stake in an elaborate ceremony ironically called an *auto-da-fé* ("act of faith").

In his sixteen-year rule, the Grand Inquisitor burned two thousand people, condemned thousands more to rot in the Inquisition's dungeons, and left a grim legacy to the church he served so ruthlessly. The Inquisition did not disappear entirely in Spain or in its colonies until 1836. By that time, hundreds of thousands had perished in flames and in dungeons, most condemned simply because their beliefs differed from approved doctrine.

The end of the Inquisition did not stop genocide in 1836 any more than the defeat of Adolf Hitler stopped it a hundred years later. The simple and sobering truth is that genocide is as old as recorded history, and as new as race wars in South Africa and "ethnic cleansing" in Bosnia and Rwanda.

17

What Causes Genocide, and How Can It Be Prevented?

Sociologists and human rights advocates have been grappling with these questions for years, without finding clear answers. There are many theories about causation and prevention, but all the experts seem to agree on one point: Society cannot afford to ignore or forget genocides of the past. "Collective denial [of genocide]," wrote Kurt Jonassohn, "amounts to saying that 'what must not be, cannot be'; also, that which is denied need not be prevented. Therefore, it is important to counteract all forms of denial and to keep the memories alive."[9]

In the name of memory, governments build monuments, human rights groups devise educational programs, and survivors bear witness to what they have seen and heard. Memory thus serves as a tribute to the dead—and a warning to the living.

3

The War Against Native Americans

History gives us a comforting distance from the pain of the victims and the guilt of the perpetrators of genocides that happened hundreds of years ago in faraway places. That comfort disappears in the case of genocides that happened not so long ago, and right here at home. For decades, American historians and political leaders have grappled with a disturbing question: Did the United States commit genocide against Native Americans?

Some say yes, citing incident after bloody incident as proof of the claim. Others say no, because there was never a focused, deliberate attempt to wipe out all the diverse Native American cultures that flourished on the American continent before the arrival of Europeans. In other words, the all-important factor of intent was not present.

One thing seems clear. By whatever name it is called, the war against Native Americans had many characteristics of genocide: dehumanization of the target group, forced marches, mass internment without due process of law, and outright extermination of thousands of men, women, and children. The California *Model Curriculum for Human Rights and Genocide* acknowledges this view in "This Sad Legacy":

> Beginning with America's first settlements, American Indians lost their land and their lives, as colonists and settlers usurped the home of the native peoples to build a new nation. Some people say the treatment of Native Americans constitutes genocide. The army sometimes deliberately spread smallpox; they warred with superior weapons, moved large populations from fertile native lands to barren deserts and attempted to destroy native cultures.[1]

The Trail of Tears

The period of the Trail of Tears officially began in 1830, when President Andrew Jackson signed the Indian Removal Act into law. Like most whites of his day, Jackson regarded Indians as less than human savages who were probably dangerous and definitely in the way. He personally signed more than ninety treaties with various tribes who agreed to leave their ancestral homelands and make the difficult journey across the "Great Waters" (the Mississippi River) to a new land that would be theirs "as long as waters run and the grass shall grow."[2]

"Thus," wrote Jackson biographer Robert V. Remini, "the tragic removal of the Indian began. . . . Often, Indians were tricked into signing away their possessions and then driven off before adequate arrangements could be initiated for an orderly migration westward. They were pressed along a 'trail of tears' to find disease, starvation, and death on the western plains."[3]

This man, whose name translates into English as "Chicken Seagull," is a Pomo Indian from the Clear Lake region of northern California. He was born in 1852, when his people were struggling to survive the influx of Anglo settlers.

Native Americans were forced to leave their homes in Mississippi, Alabama, Georgia, Tennessee, and North Carolina. In *Native American Testimony*, anthropologist Peter Nabokov tells a story that captures the hardships of those days, and the grief of those people:

> As one Choctaw community was about to move from its ancestral Mississippi forest and start the westward trek to Indian Territory, the women made a formal procession through the trees surrounding their abandoned cabins, stroking the leaves of the oak and elm trees in silent farewell.[4]

The Cherokees resisted deportation until 1838, when the United States army finally forced them to leave their woodland homes for an uncertain future on the plains. Under the command of General Winfield Scott, the military was both relentless and thorough. Historian Benson J. Lossing wrote of the event:

> The soldiers built thirteen stockades in North Carolina, Georgia, Tennessee, and Alabama. Using these as base camps, they scattered throughout the countryside with loaded rifles and fixed bayonets. As they herded Indians back toward the forts, bands of roving outlaws burned the homes, stole the livestock, robbed the graves. . . . Removal itself began during the autumn. A few early contingents had been moved out along the Tennessee River in large two-decker keelboats. The majority would travel overland. Thirteen detachments of about 1,000 each, plus 645 wagons carrying the sick and aged, departed from southeastern Tennessee.[5]

About fifteen thousand Cherokees began the journey; at least four thousand died along the way. Altogether, sixty different tribes suffered a similar fate. By the end of the deportations, as many as thirty thousand Native Americans had perished from exposure, starvation, accident, and disease.

A Peaceful, Gentle People

Native Americans on the Pacific Coast suffered a different fate. Before the whites came, dozens of small tribes, including the Pomo, Modoc, Chumash, and Yuki, lived by fishing, gathering berries and edible roots, and hunting small game. The whites dismissed them as "Digger Indians," considering them subhuman and inferior creatures who could be mistreated, enslaved, and even killed without mercy. When gold was discovered in 1848, about one hundred thousand Indians lived in California. Eleven years later, when the Gold Rush was just tattered memories and played-out mines, only thirty thousand were left; the rest had been killed by the whites, either directly or by exposure to infectious diseases. Historian Ralph Andrist wrote:

> Indians were ruthlessly driven from their tribal grounds, and when they did attempt to resist by attacking isolated miners, the prospectors hunted down all natives in the area in the same joyous fashion they would have gone after jackrabbits. Women were brutalized by gang rapes; men were captured like animals and forced to do field labor, kidnapped children were treated as slaves.[6]

Newspaper accounts of the period reflected this deep-seated contempt for Indian lives. The *Humboldt Times* (Eureka, California) carried this headline on April 11, 1863:

"Good Haul of Diggers—One White Man Killed—Thirty-eight Bucks Killed, Forty Squaws and Children Taken."[7] Just over a month later, the same newspaper stated that "the Indian

23

must be exterminated or removed. . . . This may not be the most Christianlike attitude but it is the most practical."[8]

In that climate of hatred, a ranch foreman named H. L. Hall openly boasted of killing Native Americans. In a deposition given on February 26, 1860, he told of transporting a group of captured women and children, noting that only one young boy had survived the journey: "I think all the squaws were killed because they refused to go further. We took one boy into the valley, and the infants were put out of their misery, and a girl ten years of age was killed for stubbornness."[9]

Extremists like Hall were in the minority, but even the most decent, humane settlers showed an offhand, almost casual bigotry toward Native Americans. They would call Native American men "bucks" as if they were animals, proclaim the white man's right to dominate "inferior" races, and sanction harsh punishments for even the most trivial offenses. Most of all, they would look away while Native Americans were enslaved and slaughtered.

Incident on Bloody Island

In the autumn of 1849, Native Americans near Clear Lake in northern California killed two white settlers, rancher Andrew Kelsey and his foreman, Charles Stone. The Kelsey brothers, Andrew and Benjamin, had built and run their ranch with Native-American labor. For years before the killings, the Kelseys had exploited the Pomo people, paying little or nothing for work that was always hard and sometimes dangerous, keeping women and children on the edge of starvation, dealing out brutal punishments for the smallest infraction of their rules. A neighbor, Thomas Knight, told how the Kelseys treated their Pomo workers:

The Kelseys would sometimes go out and get fifty, sixty or a hundred of these Indians, and bring them to their place, and make them work for them. They treated them badly, and did not feed them well. . . . The Indians were kept so short of food that they occasionally took a bullock and killed it themselves. . . . If the Kelseys failed to discover the special offenders, they would take any Indian they might suspect, or perhaps one at random and hang him up by the thumbs, so that his toes just touched the floor . . . and keep him there two or three days, sometimes with nothing to eat. . . . Sometimes they would kill an Indian outright on the spot for some small offence. In driving them to their place, they would shoot. . . the old or infirm ones by the wayside.[10]

In the winter of 1849, two Pomo men accidentally lost Andrew Kelsey's favorite horse during a forbidden midnight hunt. They had planned to kill a cow to feed their starving village; now they had endangered themselves and everybody else. The people knew from hard experience that Kelsey would not hesitate to brutalize dozens of Pomos for this one act. After long deliberation, the tribal council decided there was only one thing to do: Five men went to the ranch house early the next morning and killed Stone and Kelsey.

Anti-Native-American feeling ran so high after the killing that Major General Persifor F. Smith dispatched troops under the command of Captain Nathaniel Lyon, with orders "to waste no time in parley, to ascertain with certainty the offenders, and to strike them promptly and heavily."[11]

When the soldiers attacked their village, the Pomos escaped and sought refuge on a small, tree-covered island in the northern part of Clear Lake. Soon called Bloody Island, it became what Captain Lyon would later call "a perfect slaughter pen."[12]

25

Lyon set up a simple but clever trap. While cavalry attacked from the nearest shore, boatloads of infantrymen approached the island from the rear, trapping the Pomos. The maneuver worked with devastating results: More than a hundred men, women, and children died that day, and dozens more were wounded.

Bloody Island was not the first mass murder of Native Americans on the Pacific Coast. It would not be the last. By the 1860s, groups of Native-American-hating vigilantes had turned mass slaughter into a business. Walter Jarboe, one of the most brutal of the vigilante leaders, killed more than three hundred Native Americans in his five months as leader of the quasi-military Eel River Rangers. His favorite method was to torch whole villages, burning men, women, and children alive in their huts. He justified these murderous forays with the familiar cry of the genocidal bigot:

> The Ukas are without doubt, the most degraded, filthy, miserable thieving lot of any living thing that comes under the head of and rank of human beings. . . . It may be that nothing short of extermination will suffice to rid the Country of them to make them cease their thieving and murderous course.[13]

The Horse-and-Buffalo Tribes

Brutal men like Walter Jarboe were not limited to the West Coast. On the great Central Plains another struggle between whites and Native Americans took on the aspects of genocide. For men such as Colonel John M. Chivington and Generals William T. Sherman and Philip Sheridan, wholesale destruction was one sure way to solve the "Indian problem" on the western frontier.

Chivington was perhaps the most cruel of all the commanders. He was powerfully built, with a barrel chest, grim, humorless eyes, and manners to match that imposing appearance. He was a lay preacher in the Methodist Church, a would-be politician, and a zealot who possessed absolute certainty that his beliefs were superior to all others. "To the Indians," wrote historian Dee Brown, "he appeared like a great bearded bull buffalo with a glint of furious madness in his eyes."[14]

It was this bull buffalo of a man who attacked a peaceful Cheyenne encampment at Sand Creek, Colorado, despite the fact that Chief Black Kettle had placed his people under the protection of the army at Fort Lyon. On November 29, 1864, at first light, 750 men descended upon the camp. Their orders from Chivington were clear and brutal: "Kill and scalp all, big and little; nits make lice."[15]

George Bent, the son of a white father and a Cheyenne mother, was camped with his Cheyenne relations when the attack began. He later reported:

> All was confusion and noise, men, women and children rushing out of the lodges partly dressed; women and children screaming at the sight of the troops; men running back into the lodges for their arms. . . . I looked toward the chief's lodge and saw that Black Kettle had a large American flag tied to the end of a long lodgepole and he was standing in front of his lodge, holding the pole, with the flag fluttering in the gray light of the winter dawn. I heard him call to the people not to be afraid, that the soldiers would not hurt them; then the troops opened fire from two sides of the camp.[16]

Chivington's men rode into the camp, shooting down women and children, impaling babies in their mothers' arms.

No one knows how many died that day, but estimates place the figure around 150, mostly women and children.

Though Chivington boasted of his "accomplishment," other white Americans were shocked by his excesses. Four years after the event, military investigators forced the colonel to resign his commission to avoid court-martial. This official disavowal of the colonel and his deeds was too little too late, for the damage had already been done. In a single morning of blood and gore, John Chivington set in motion a conflict that would not end until the massacre at Wounded Knee on December 29, 1890.

The Road to Wounded Knee

In the years between Sand Creek and Wounded Knee, official policy toward Native Americans wavered between extermination and containment. Shortly before his election to the presidency, Ulysses S. Grant vowed to protect white settlers on the plains even "if the extermination of every Indian tribe was necessary to secure such a result."[17]

With the threat of total annihilation hanging over their heads, the Plains tribes were forced onto reservations and systematically stripped of their culture. Native Americans were forbidden to speak their own languages, observe their own festivals, or practice their own religious traditions. Parents were forced to send their children to "Indian schools," boarding schools where young Cheyenne, Sioux, Navajo, Arapaho, and Apache learned the ways of white culture.

The process was well under way by 1888, when a Paiute named Wovoka brought a message of hope to Native Americans everywhere: By performing the mystical and magical Ghost Dance, they could restore lost comrades to life, reclaim their

Despite Anglo attempts to abolish Native-American culture, many tribes held on to their ancestral traditions. In this 1923 photo, a group of Pomo Indians are shown preparing for a ritual dance. The handmade traditional costumes required many hours to complete.

ancestral ways, and force the white conquerors from their lands. Desperate starving people danced Wovoka's dance and sang Wovoka's songs:

> My Father, have pity on me!
> I have nothing to eat,
> I am dying of thirst—
> Everything is gone! [18]

Nervous whites tried to end the Ghost Dance, first with lectures, then with laws, and finally with guns. The massacre at Wounded Knee began as an attempt to stop the Sioux from performing the Ghost Dance. The Sioux holy man Black Elk was a young boy on December 29. Years later, he recalled the horror in words that became the epitaph for a people and a way of life that had thrived for generations before the coming of Europeans, with their deadly weapons, their greed for land, and their contempt for Native-American ways.

> I did not know then how much was ended. When I look back now from this high hill of my old age, I can still see the butchered women and children lying heaped and scattered all along the crooked gulch as plain as when I saw them with eyes still young. And I can see that something else died there in the bloody mud, and was buried in the blizzard. A people's dream died there. It was a beautiful dream. [19]

4

The Armenian Genocide

On April 24, 1915, Turkish police in Constantinople (modern Istanbul), the capital of the Ottoman Empire, descended on Armenian neighborhoods to arrest community leaders, professional people, and intellectuals. Six hundred prominent Armenians were dragged from their homes and thrown into jail. Three days later, they disappeared, never to be heard from again. With these natural leaders gone, the Turks had no trouble rounding up the rest of the Armenians in Constantinople. Five thousand people were taken from their homes and were forced to march in a long, grim procession toward an unknown destination. Thousands more followed, from other cities and towns throughout the Ottoman Empire. Few of them would survive the journey. Their crime: Being Armenians.

World War I raged through Europe, and the Ottoman Empire (of which only Turkey remains) found itself allied

World War I soldiers wearing gas masks. Chemical weapons added a dimension of random, invisible terror to the conflict, overshadowing world concerns for Armenian deportees.

with Germany against Russia, its troublesome neighbor to the east. Armenians lived on both sides of that border, a fact that made the government uneasy. Not only were the Ottoman Armenians linked to their Russian brethren, they lived among the Turks as a people apart—Christians in a Muslim land, speaking their own language, and maintaining their own customs.

In the mind of the ruthless young Ottoman minister of war, Enver Pasha (*Pasha* was a title of rank, placed after the name of high-ranking civilian or military officials), that made them security risks. As the most powerful of the triumvirate (the three leaders ruling the empire), Enver had broad authority to move against anyone who might pose a threat to the empire—and he did not hesitate to use that authority. With the aid and consent of his corulers, Talaat Pasha and Jemal Pasha, Enver launched the horror that began on that spring morning in 1915. Armenians all over the world still commemorate April 24 as a day of deep mourning, the beginning of genocide.

A Deadly Legacy

The groundwork for that genocide had been part of the very foundation of Ottoman society. Discriminatory laws classed Armenians and other Christians as second-class citizens in a Muslim nation. They were "tolerated *infidels*," who could not own guns, intermarry with Muslims, or testify against a Muslim in court. Despite these official restrictions, many Armenians rose to positions of wealth and influence within the empire.

This success was almost their undoing when Sultan Abdul Hamid II came to the Ottoman throne in 1876. He was a fearful, suspicious leader who isolated himself from society and worried constantly about sabotage, assassination, and other acts of high treason. Fear made him so vicious and repressive that he triggered the very opposition he was trying to prevent. In the 1890s, Armenians began demanding their rights. Some simply wanted greater freedom and equality under the laws of the empire, while others pressed for an independent Armenian state.

Hamid saw these Armenian freedom groups as a threat, and he acted accordingly. He "responded with the sly policy of exploiting the differences between Moslem and Christian," wrote historian Lord Kinross.

> Using the Kurds as a deliberate instrument of division . . . he sanctioned their attacks on the Armenians by starting, in 1891, to recruit an armed force of irregulars from among the Kurdish tribesmen. Named the *Hamidiye*, the "men of the Sultan," they were formed into cavalry regiments which by the end of 1892 comprised in all some fifteen thousand men, and which continued to increase year by year. . . . They spread fear through the open avowal that their official task was to suppress the Armenians, and that they were assured of legal immunity for any acts of oppression against the Christian population.[1]

Between 1894 and 1896, these troops killed an estimated three hundred thousand Armenians, but the attacks were part of a wider policy of repression that affected the whole empire. The special nature of actions against Armenians slipped by unnoticed. In time, Hamid's tyranny began to rankle even his Muslim subjects, and in 1909 he was deposed by the Young Turks, a group of dissident army officers. They pledged to build a liberal, Western-style democracy upon the ruins of the dying empire.

One idealistic young officer hailed a new era of freedom and equality throughout the land: "Henceforth we are all brothers," he said. "There are no longer Bulgars, Greeks, Roumans, Jews, Moslems; under the same blue sky we are all equal, we glory in being Ottomans."[2] That officer's name was Enver Bey; he would soon carry the exalted title of Pasha.

The Triumvirate

While the Young Turks dethroned a sultan and tried to establish a new government, the nations of Europe pursued a course that would soon lead to war. The Ottoman Empire found itself at the crossroads of conflict, with no allies on either side and a weakened government unable to unify the country, let alone to deal with the worsening international situation. In this climate of uncertainty, a new and deadly strain of ultranationalism took root, replacing the Ottoman ideal of equality.

> The Young Turks . . . began to develop a unique philosophy, one that stressed special Turkish history and a special future. This new Philosophy . . . was a Turkish racial ideology. Muslims were considered superior to Christians, and Turks deserved a 'privileged position' in the Empire over all other nationalities, including the Arab Muslims.[3]

By the time World War I began in August 1914, the Young Turks had successfully transformed Turkish nationalism into a growing anti-Armenian movement.

The Beginnings of Genocide

Genocides always seem to happen in times of war for a reason: People grow accustomed to death and horror. They dehumanize the enemy to make the killing easier, and measure patriots by the depth of their hatred. It is not especially difficult to hide mass executions within casualty reports, to disguise death marches as the "relocation" of endangered civilians, and to commit the most unspeakable atrocities in the name of God, Country, or National Security.

Historian Richard G. Hovannisian summed up this relationship between genocide and war: "The sad truth must be recorded that it was well nigh impossible in 1915 to get worked up about mass tragedy, any kind of mass tragedy, in remote forgotten corners of the earth. The world was at war. Millions were being killed and maimed everywhere."[4]

The Turks were so frightened of the European war on their doorstep that no one thought to protest when the government ordered all Armenian soldiers to surrender their weapons and to leave their units. "These former soldiers . . . were transformed into road [workers] and pack animals," wrote United States ambassador Henry Morgenthau, who was in Constantinople at the time.

> Army supplies of all kinds were loaded on their backs, and stumbling under the burdens and driven by the whips and bayonets of the Turks, they were forced to drag their weary bodies into the mountains of the Caucasus. . . . They were given only scraps of food; if they felt sick they were left where they had dropped. . . . Here and there squads of 50 or 100 men would be taken, bound together in groups of four, and then marched out to a secluded spot a short distance from the village. Suddenly the sound of rifle shots would fill the air. . . . In cases that came to my attention, the murderers had added a refinement to their victims' sufferings by compelling them to dig their graves before being shot.[5]

The Armenian genocide had begun.

A Journey to Nowhere

The pattern established in Constantinople continued in Armenian communities all over the empire. After the leaders were executed and the former soldiers were disarmed, the rest of the people were taken from their homes and forced to march. "Along the way some were killed outright, and tens of thousands more died of dehydration, hunger, exhaustion, exposure, and disease," wrote Donald E. Miller and Lorna Touryan Miller in *Survivors: An Oral History of the Armenian Genocide.* "Although deportation might not have been as technologically sophisticated as gas chambers and ovens, it was equally effective at destroying human life."[6]

Kerop Bedoukian was nine years old when the deportations began in Sivas, a city with a large and thriving Armenian population. He and his family first learned of the deportations when the town crier walked through their street, calling out the news: All Armenians had to be ready to leave in three days. Where they were going, or why, nobody would say.

On the appointed day, everyone assembled as ordered— old people grumbling about having come to such a state, mothers carrying infants in their arms, children restless with uncertainty. Mounted armed guards, with fierce, unfriendly eyes rode at the front and back of this improbable caravan.

At the beginning of the march, some families had wagons, animals, food supplies, and money, but these were soon stolen by marauders or conscripted by the caravan guards. Before long, most people had lost everything but a few shreds of clothing and whatever small valuables they could hide from robbers. "The caravan stretched out for miles," wrote Bedoukian, "wagon wheels squeaking, guards on horseback galloping back and forth, whipping anyone who straggled behind. . . .

37

Armenian refugees flooded into the United States and other countries after World War I. This once prosperous family arrived in San Francisco on March 8, 1919, still numbed and frightened by the strangeness of their surroundings.

At the rear, the guards threatened the slow marchers, who, in their effort to avoid punishment, crowded the marchers in front, and the line doubled and redoubled, spreading out on both sides of the road."[7]

Dismal as this was, worse lay in store. Death became a constant reality on the march. Every day, more people died—some at the hands of guards or marauders, others from exhaustion, starvation, or disease. Kerop Bedoukian described the experience:

> Common sense told everyone that there was no particular destination. . . . That the end would come only by death was the accepted and logical fact. . . . Water had to be used with care, since the marchers were steered away from sources of water. The rivers or brooks that we crossed were usually contaminated with cadavers, swollen and worm-eaten under the blazing-hot sun. Wherever there was water, the surrounding space was covered with bodies in all stages of decay.[8]

Other survivors of the deportation marches told much the same story. Death was a constant presence among the deportees, and it came in many forms. The caravans were repeatedly attacked by Kurdish tribesmen, Turkish villagers, and the roving bands of murderers and other criminals who had been released from prison on condition that they serve as execution squads for the Ottoman army. Two doctors, Nazim and Shakir, betrayed their oath of healing to play a key role in organizing the execution squads, which operated under orders of the Ministries of Justice and Interior.

Under the policy of death by deportation, more than a million Armenians were killed by the time the Ottoman Empire and its allies were defeated in 1918. The dying still was not over. Hundreds of thousands starved to death in the famine of 1918 to 1920, or died at the hands of vengeful Turks when they tried to return to their homes. Another million were exiled, spreading over the world as refugees. Of the two million Armenians who had lived in the Ottoman empire, scarcely a hundred thousand remained.

Tribunals and inquiries were conducted, and world leaders made public statements of outrage and shock. A Turkish military court found Enver, Talaat, Jemal, and Nazim guilty of war crimes and sentenced them to death, but the sentence was never carried out. The infamous triumvirate and the organizer of execution squads escaped the country at the end of the war. Thousands of other war criminals never stood trial; they continued their jobs and their lives as if nothing had happened. Within a few months, the trials themselves were discontinued and the world forgot the Armenians.

The survivors and their families could not forget, and their descendants have not forgotten either. Each year, on April 24, Armenians observe a day of mourning for the victims of this first genocide of the twentieth century.

5

Forced Famine in Ukraine

In the interval between world wars, the Soviet Union used starvation the way the Young Turks had used deportation—as a weapon of genocide. *Shtuchnyi holod,* ("the manmade famine,") the Ukrainians called it. By order of Soviet leader Joseph Stalin, millions of Ukrainian peasants starved to death in the famine of 1932 to 1933.

One of the most coldly brutal tyrants in history, Stalin understood mass psychology and mass murder. Killing was a tool; properly used it could eliminate enemies, terrorize survivors into submission, and overwhelm outsiders beyond their ability to cope or intervene. "When one man dies it's a tragedy," Stalin once said. "When thousands die it's statistics."[1]

By sheer weight of numbers, Ukraine's tragedy was so terrible, its death toll so huge, that people who might have protested were rendered numb. In the face of such devastation, protest seemed useless, and the world was silent, as Stalin had known it would be.

Targeting the Enemy

The man the world knew as Joseph Stalin was born Iosif Vissarionovich Dzhugashvili in Georgia, on December 21, 1879. He became a revolutionary in his early twenties, running afoul of the law so often that he used half a dozen false names trying to escape arrest. He finally settled on Stalin, from the Russian *stal* (steel). The name suited him.

As second in command to Vladimir Ilyich Lenin, the guiding force of the Russian Revolution, Stalin helped to stamp out Tsarist despotism and to replace it with the so-called dictatorship of the *proletariat* (the working class). Collectivization of labor and public ownership of property became the social ideal, and the government was run by a committee of Communist party officials, known as the Politburo.

Stalin came to power after Lenin's death in 1924, inheriting a government that was still struggling to control an unwieldy empire. The new premier soon turned his attention toward Ukraine, the largest and most troublesome of the non-Russian Soviet republics. The Ukrainians were a fiercely independent people, given to ignoring directives from Moscow and stubbornly maintaining their individualistic, agrarian way of life.

That independent spirit made them a problem. At a time when Stalin wanted to build a strong industrial base, they clung to their rural peasant traditions. At a time when he wanted to abolish private ownership of land, they refused to surrender their farms. In short, the Ukrainians had become a threat to the revolution.

42

Thousands of Eastern Orthodox priests, professors, writers, and government officials were dragged from their homes and were executed or forced onto trains bound for the frozen waste of Siberia. With the leadership out of the way, Stalin turned toward another target: land-owning (and therefore supposedly rich) peasants who resisted the whole idea of collectivized farming and state ownership of the land. Lenin had dubbed them *kulaks*, deliberately choosing a name that people would associate with greed and cunning.

"In Russian," wrote Nobel Prize-winning writer Aleksandr Solzhenitsyn:

> a *kulak* is a miserly, dishonest rural trader who grows rich not by his own labor but through someone else's, through usury [moneylending at inflated—and illegal—rates of interest] and operating as a middleman . . . . By 1930 *all strong peasants in general* were being so called—all peasants strong in management, strong in work, or even strong merely in convictions.[2]

Under Stalin's orders, the Soviets moved relentlessly through the entire fabric of society. First came the prosperous, land-owning peasants who ran their large farms as businesses. When they were gone, Stalin produced more victims by the simple tactic of redefining *kulak* to include anyone who owned a plot of land and tended a modest family garden. Next, he moved beyond *kulak* to identify another enemy, this one more hidden, and therefore more dangerous to the revolution, than any of the others.

"A new word was needed for all these new victims as a class—and it was born," wrote Aleksandr Solzhenitsyn. "By this time it had no 'social' or 'economic' content whatsoever, but it had a marvelous sound—*podkulachnik*—'a person aiding the kulaks.' In other words, I consider you an accomplice of the enemy. And that finishes you! The most tattered landless laborer in the countryside could quite easily be labeled a *podkulachnik.*"[3]

According to the Ukrainian National Association, "200,000 families were 'de-kulakized' or dispossessed of all land. By the summer of 1932, 69.5 percent of all Ukrainian farm families and 80 percent of all farm land had been forcibly collectivized."[4] Not even this satisfied Stalin, especially when grain producing collective farms fell short of government quotas, just at the time that agricultural prices tumbled in the world market.

In his study of the famine, James Mace considered its political significance: "The Soviet Union, whose entire plan of development was [based] on paying for imported capital goods with the proceeds from agricultural sales, found that a given machine cost far more grain than had previously been the case."[5] Stalin used this crisis to tighten his grip on Ukraine. He realized that he could get more grain to pay for industrialization and starve the Ukrainian peasants into submission at the same time.

Death by Design

On December 27, 1929, Stalin announced his intention to liquidate the kulaks as a class and to force the surviving Ukrainian peasants onto government-owned collective farms. That same winter, almost ten million men, women, and children were deported to Siberian labor camps.

In July 1932, Stalin issued the decree that set the famine into motion. It ordered Ukrainian farmers to produce an impossible 6.6 million tons of grain in the next harvest. Soviet novelist Vasily Grossman observed that "the decree required that the peasants of Ukraine . . . be put to death by starvation, put to death along with their little children."[6]

On August 7, 1932, another law declared every crop in Ukraine to be government property. "Anyone who so much as gleaned an ear of grain or bit the root off a sugar beet was to be considered an enemy of the people subject to execution. . . ."[7]

After the 1932 harvest, which fell far short of quota, the government seized the entire grain crop, and then dispatched special brigades to search out and confiscate private supplies of food.

Like the execution squads that had preyed upon Armenians less than twenty years earlier, the Soviet special brigades included ex-convicts, terrorists, and other unsavory types; this time the leaders were Communist party functionaries. According to historian Clarence Manning, these brigades:

> entered the villages and made . . . searches of the houses and barns of every peasant. They dug up the earth and broke into the walls of buildings and stoves in which the peasants tried to hide their last handfuls of food. They even . . . took specimens of fecal matter from the toilets in an effort to learn by analysis whether the peasants had stolen government property and were eating grain.[8]

In addition to this brutal search and seizure, the government imposed strict travel bans to prevent people from leaving their blighted villages in search of food. "This ban on free travel by starving farmers was an added cause of the deaths of hundreds of people in the surrounding districts," stated survivor Stephan Dubovyk, a train conductor stationed in the town of Osnova. "Four hundred people died of starvation in the village of Borshchivka, 350 in the village of Blahodyrivka . . . 1,200 in the collective farm 'Red Star,'

45

1,800 in the small towns of Boromlia, and so on in all the villages, hamlets and towns throughout Ukraine."[9]

The peasants resisted as best they could, hiding food and opposing the brigades at every turn. In spite of these acts of resistance, winter brought famine, and people began to die.

The Great Hunger

As that winter of 1933 wore on, so many Ukrainians died, by the hundreds of thousands, that disposing of the bodies became a problem. Children "buried" parents where they fell, covering the bodies over with a few handfuls of dirt or perhaps some straw or fallen leaves. Parents left dead or dying babies by the roadside. A railroad engineer recalled a particularly chilling discovery at the Kavkaz station in the Northern Caucasus:

> Every morning at a fixed hour before dawn two mysterious trains would leave in the direction of Mineralni Vody and Rostov. The trains were empty and consisted of five to ten freight cars each. Between two and four hours later the trains would return, stop for a certain time at a small way station, and then proceed on a dead-end spur towards a former ballast quarry. While the trains stopped in Kavkaz, or on a side track, all cars were locked, appeared loaded and were closely guarded by the *NKVD* [the Soviet secret police].
>
> Nobody paid any attention to the mysterious trains at first: I did not either. . . . But one day [the] conductor . . . called me quietly and took me to the trains, saying: "I wanted to show you what is in the cars." He opened the door of one car slightly. I looked in and almost swooned at the sight I saw. It was full of corpses, piled at random.[10]

Stalin's Legacy

In the midst of this gruesome reality, the Soviet government hid the truth of the developing genocide. In the eyes of the world, Stalin attributed the famine to "conditions beyond human control." Prices had dropped, crops were poor, and the entire world economy was caught in the throes of a great depression. It was misfortune and not malice that caused the Ukrainian difficulties, Stalin claimed, and he went to a great deal of trouble to preserve that fiction.

The government made certain that foreign visitors saw only what the authorities wanted them to see. According to a 1974 article in the underground newspaper *Ukrainian Herald,* "The cities, especially those like Kharkov and Kiev, were carefully cleaned of the starving and the dead peasants, so that foreign correspondents and political figures could be shown the clean streets, thus rectifying the 'slanderous fabrications circulated by bourgeois propaganda.'"[11]

The Soviet people either accepted the official government line, or pretended to accept it out of fear and helplessness. Many wanted so desperately to believe in the justice and decency of the Soviet system that they turned a blind eye to the horror. "We were deceived because we wanted to be deceived," said dissident Petro Grigorenko, a former general in the Soviet army. "We believed so strongly in communism that we [would] accept any crime if it was glossed over with the least little bit of Communist phraseology. . . ."[12]

No one knows how many died in the famine of 1932 to 1933. Some say five million; some say ten. The only certainty is that millions died because Joseph Stalin saw them as a threat to the Communist ideal. Because it was purposefully engineered, and perpetrated against an identifiable national group, the Ukrainian famine falls within the United Nations definition of genocide: an action committed "with intent to destroy, in whole or in part, a national, ethnic, racial or religious group."[13]

6

The Holocaust

On January 30, 1933, a new chancellor, the chief minister of state, took office in Germany. To a nation still demoralized by its defeat in World War I, he spoke with fire and conviction about the German "master race," promising conquest, glory, and *lebensraum* ("living space") for those with the vision to follow him. That chancellor's name was Adolf Hitler.

Through wholesale violence and an endless barrage of propaganda, he remolded Germany in the image of his National Socialist German Workers'—Nazi—party. The word *Nazi* comes from the first two syllables of *Nazional,* the German word for "national."

The Ways of Hatred

From the beginning, Hitler was openly racist, proclaiming the superiority of the so-called Aryan peoples and denouncing

Jews as dangerous and deadly vermin who would surely destroy Germany if Germany did not destroy them first. According to Nazi racial theory, an Aryan was a person of pure Germanic blood. Anti-Semitism—prejudice and discrimination against Jews—had existed in Europe for hundreds of years, but Adolf Hitler exploited it in ways that even Grand Inquisitor Torquemada could not have imagined. The propaganda war he began in 1933 led in time to the Holocaust—the systematic killing that decimated European Jewry.

As Hitler's hate campaign took hold, ordinary Germans, who considered themselves decent, upright citizens, began to avoid Jewish neighbors, coworkers, and even friends. They boycotted Jewish businesses and proudly displayed stickers labelled "German Firm" in their own shop windows.

"Bring up the Jewish question again and again and again, unceasingly," Hitler told his propagandists:

> Every emotional aversion, however slight, must be exploited ruthlessly. As a basic rule among the education professions the Jewish questions should be discussed from the standpoints of the findings of the Science of Race, of higher ethics, etc. While among members of the labouring classes one must seize on the purely emotional; the emotional aversion to Jews is to be heightened by all possible means.[1]

Jews as Outcasts

On September 15, 1935, the Nuremberg Laws, named after the German town where they were formulated, stripped Jews of their German citizenship and civil rights. By 1938, Jews had been banned from nearly every aspect of German life:

Before the Nazis overran Hungary, Nador Livia was a famous actress on the Budapest stage. Like thousands of other Jews, she was imprisoned simply because of her heritage. This photo was taken at Gusen concentration camp.

government, civil service, journalism, radio, teaching, theater, films, stock exchanges, medicine, and law.

At this stage, Hitler proceeded cautiously with his anti-Jewish measures, testing the waters of world opinion while he gathered military and political strength. According to many who lived through those prewar years, Hitler possessed a diabolical sense of timing; he always seemed to know just how far he could go without provoking organized resistance.

This timing was critical to the Nazi's plan. Milton Mayer wrote about this timing in his book, *They Thought They Were Free*:

> If the last and worst act of the whole regime had come immediately after the first and smallest, thousands, yes millions, would have been sufficiently shocked—if, let us say, the gassing of the Jews in '43 had come immediately after the "German Firm" stickers on the windows of non-Jewish shops in '33. But of course this isn't the way it happens. In between come all the hundreds of little steps, some of them imperceptible, each of them preparing you not to be shocked by the next. Step C is not so much worse than Step B, and, if you do not make a stand at Step B, why should you at Step C? And so on to Step D.[2]

As the Nazis occupied new territory in their quest for lebensraum, the plight of the Jews grew even more desperate. Tens of thousands fled Nazi terror, becoming refugees in a world that was already preparing for a war that seemed inevitable.

Chronicles of Suffering

At dawn on September 1, 1939, Germany invaded Poland, and World War II began. With troops, tanks, and aerial bombardment, the Nazis crushed Polish resistance, and then rolled over the rest of Europe like a great, dark wave. As one country after another fell to the occupying armies, whole communities of Jews were trapped behind ever advancing enemy lines. The Nazis dealt with them immediately, executing thousands outright and herding the rest into ghettos to await a slower, more agonizing end.

Much of what we know of life in these ghettos comes from the writings of people like Emanuel Ringelblum, a forty-one-year-old historian who lived in the Jewish ghetto of Warsaw, Poland's capital city. Ringelblum was the head of a group calling itself the *Oneg Shabbat* (Hebrew for "Sabbath joy") *Circle*, which existed for the sole purpose of recording the life and death of the Warsaw ghetto for future generations. To protect Ringelblum's work from the Nazis, Circle members put the manuscripts into tin boxes and milk cans and buried them in the ghetto. Part of the archive was unearthed in 1946; the rest was found in 1950.

Ringelblum's Oneg Shabbat diaries related a nightmarish account of starvation, disease, and torture, of people existing in lice-infested rooms or freezing to death in the winter streets. By spring 1941, five or six hundred Jews were dying of hunger every week. "Death lies in every street," Ringelblum wrote on May 11, 1941. "The children are no longer afraid of death. In one courtyard, the children played a game tickling a corpse."[3]

While Ringelblum recorded the stark images of the Warsaw ghetto, a teenage diarist in Amsterdam tried to make sense of her own wartime experiences. Anne Frank was the youngest daughter of Jewish businessman Otto Frank, who moved his family into hiding when Nazi troops occupied Holland. After arranging for Christian friends to bring them food and other necessities, the Franks settled down to the bleak, even boring task of waiting out the war. With her

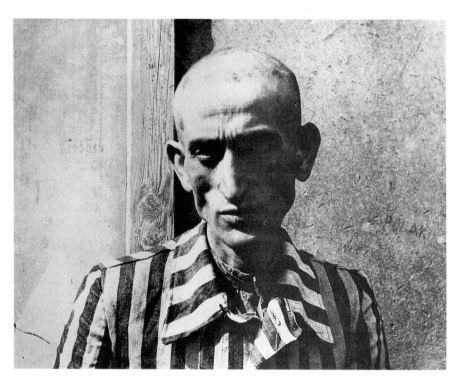

One of the "living dead" of Dachau. The camp was filled with people in advanced stages of starvation or disease. They worked until they could work no more, and then they were killed.

horizons narrowed to the size and shape of a hidden apartment, Anne used the diary she called Kitty to come to grips with the minor crises and major questions of her life. *The Diary of a Young Girl* became a testament to the hope and quiet endurance of ordinary people trapped in an extraordinary situation.

The Killing Squads

When the Nazis attacked the Soviet Union in June 1941, they entered a new phase in their genocidal program, creating special execution squads (called *Einsatzgruppen*) that were trained for a single task: killing Jews. This they did in the most brutal way imaginable; they would round up all the Jews in a city or a village, make them strip naked, march them into a ditch, and shoot them where they stood. If there was not a suitably deep ditch in the vicinity, the Einsatzgruppen would force the condemned Jews to dig their own mass grave before they were executed. More than a million Jews perished this way, along with thousands of Russian Communists and other "enemies of the Reich."

This sort of personalized, face-to-face slaughter took its toll. Many members of the Einsatzgruppen, "unable to endure wading through blood any longer, had committed suicide," wrote Auschwitz Commandant Rudolph Höss. "Some had even gone mad." Most of them "had to rely on alcohol when carrying out their horrible work."[4]

Having discovered that Einsatzgruppen could not kill as quickly as Hitler demanded, the Nazi leadership sought a new and more efficient method of dealing with what they called "the Jewish question."

55

The Final Solution

On January 20, 1942, in the Berlin suburb of Wannsee, Reinhard Heydrich, the officer who had engineered Kristallnacht in 1938, called a conference of high-level officials. According to notes of that conference, Heydrich began by informing the group that he had been appointed "*Plenipotentiary* [an official empowered to represent the government] for the Preparation of the Final Solution of the European Jewish Question."[5]

He made it clear that "final" also meant "total": The Nazi hierarchy was determined to eliminate all eleven million European Jews, even those in neutral and unconquered countries.

> By the end of January 1942, the Germans needed only to establish the apparatus of total destruction: death camps in remote areas, rolling stock, timetables . . . and then to rely upon the tacit, unspoken, unrecorded connivance of thousands of people: administrators and bureaucrats who would do their duty, organize round-ups, supervise detention centres, coordinate schedules, and send local Jews on their way to a distant, "unknown destination," to "work camps" . . . to "resettlement" in "the East."[6]

To carry out the mandate of Wannsee, the Nazis built elaborate killing centers, equipped with gas chambers that looked like shower rooms and crematoria that operated around the clock. These death camps became the most infamous and unforgettable symbol of the Holocaust. Behind their walls, mass murder became a passionless, impersonal, and efficient process.

In the ghettos, unsuspecting Jews were selected for "relocation" and were told that they would be living in work camps where conditions were comfortable, if not luxurious, and there was food enough for everyone. An endless parade of trains chugged through occupied Europe, taking carloads of Jews to the death camps.

Even there, the illusion continued for a time. At first, gas chambers were disguised as pleasant little bath houses, surrounded by flower beds and well-kept lawns. As the prisoners disembarked from their trains, they were greeted by an orchestra playing cheerful, sprightly tunes. The concert continued while the new arrivals were divided into two groups; one was sent to a slave labor camp, the other straight to the gas chamber.

The Specter of Death

In his book *Man's Search for Meaning*, psychiatrist and Holocaust survivor Viktor Frankl recalled his own arrival at Auschwitz:

> We were told to leave our luggage in the train and . . . file past a senior SS officer . . . [who] assumed an attitude of careless ease, supporting his right elbow with his left hand. His right hand was lifted, and with the forefinger of that hand he pointed leisurely to the right or to the left. None of us had the slightest idea of the sinister meaning behind that little movement of a man's finger, pointing now to the right and now to the left.[7]

Ninety percent of Frankl's transport went to the left—and to their deaths.

In Auschwitz, as many as six thousand people were gassed every day. The crematoria worked round the clock, dislodging a foul-smelling cloud of smoke and human ashes into the skies over the camp. The killing did not stop even when the fortunes of war turned against Germany. At a time when the Nazis needed men and supplies at every front, Hitler diverted scarce resources to the genocide. Trains ran day and night,

This grisly scene is part of a set of seven photos taken at Dachau. Apparently, an enterprising former inmate sold copies to American soldiers who wanted documentary proof of the atrocities they had discovered.

transporting Jews from ghettos to death camps. All over occupied Europe, the Nazis hunted down Jews with renewed zeal, conducting surprise raids at all hours of the day and night.

In August 1944, Anne Frank and her family were captured in one of these raids and deported to the camps. Only her father, Otto, survived. After the war, he returned to the hiding place in Amsterdam, where he found Anne's diary. That slim little book with its youthful musings was all he had left of his youngest daughter. Anne herself died at the Bergen-Belsen concentration camp, possibly in January 1945. She was fifteen years old.

In one of her last entries, Anne came to terms with her own inability to understand all that had happened. Millions of words have been written by people seeking to analyze and explain the Holocaust. Anne's willingness to move beyond the need for answers and get on with the business of living stands as a touching tribute to the resilience of the human spirit.

Saturday, 15 July, 1944

Dear Kitty,

Is it true then that grownups have a more difficult time here than we do? No, I know it isn't. It's twice as hard for us young ones to hold our ground . . . in a time when all ideals are being shattered and destroyed, when people are showing their worst side, and do not know whether to believe in truth and right and God. . . . It's really a wonder that I haven't dropped all my ideals, because they seem so absurd and impossible to carry out. Yet I keep them, because in spite of everything I still believe that people are really good at heart. I simply can't build my hopes on a foundation consisting of confusion, misery, and death. I see the world gradually being turned into a wilderness. I hear the ever approaching

After liberation, survivors often passed through refugee centers on the way to reclaiming their lives. This six-year-old war orphan is waiting to be transported from Buchenwald to a refugee center in Switzerland.

thunder, which will destroy us too, I can feel the sufferings of millions and yet, if I look up into the heavens, I think that it will all come right, that this cruelty too will end, and that peace and tranquility will return again.

In the meantime, I must uphold my ideals, for perhaps the time will come when I shall be able to carry them out.

Yours, Anne[8]

The Holocaust claimed lives on a scale never before seen in human history. Its victims were not casualties of war who died on battlefields and in bombing raids. They were civilians selected for death because of their Jewish heritage. It is estimated that between 65 and 70 percent of all European Jews perished, most in death factories like Auschwitz-Birkenau and Treblinka.

7

The "Other" Holocaust

Adolf Hitler launched the 1939 invasion of Poland with a speech to his commanding officers:

> Our strength is our quickness and brutality. . . . Genghis Khan had millions of women and children killed by his own will and with a [happy] heart. History sees in him only a great state builder. What weak western European civilization thinks about me does not matter. . . . I have sent to the east only my "Death Head Units," with the order to kill without mercy all men, women, and children of Polish race or language. Only in such a way will we win the vital space we need.[1]

When some people expressed concern about world opinion, Hitler reminded them of recent history: "Who still talks nowadays of the extermination of the Armenians?"[2]

After the Death Head Units had decimated the Poles and had broken their will to resist, the Nazis planned to use the survivors as slave laborers. In Hitler's perverse reality, Jews were like cancer cells eating away at a healthy body; the only cure was to annihilate them—down to the last man, woman, and child. Poles, Russians, Gypsies, and anyone else who did not fit the Aryan ideal, were *untermenschen* ("subhumans") existing for no other purpose than to serve the German "master race." Those who ceased to be useful would be killed without mercy or remorse.

To justify the extermination and enslavement of Slavs and Gypsies, the Propaganda Ministry dehumanized them with ethnic slurs and simplistic labels: Poles were stupid; Russians and Ukrainians, brutish; Gypsies, tramps and thieves. In January 1940, a nationally distributed memo called upon the German press to help spread the hate:

> Articles dealing with Poland must express the instinctive revulsion of the German people against everything which is Polish. Articles and news items must be drawn up in such a way as to transform this instinctive revulsion into a lasting revulsion. This should be done, not by special articles, but by scattering phrases here and there in the text.[3]

The War Against the Poles

The Nazis overran Poland without fear of world reprisals and immediately began exterminating intellectuals and community leaders. Thousands of scholars, teachers, and priests were executed during those first bloody weeks of German occupation. Then came the farmers and shopkeepers, the students, craftsmen, and elderly folk. Altogether, three million Polish civilians were executed or worked to death by their Nazi conquerors.

Priests were a special target, because of their commitment to moral and spiritual values that Hitler considered weak and

The fate of people Hitler classed as *untermenschen* was brutal in the extreme. The body of this victim, who was burned to death by SS troops, is still in the position in which he died.

unworthy. Slavic priests not only served a church that Hitler had vowed to "crush like a toad," but belonged to a nationality that was "ordained by Providence to be slaves to the Aryan race, a fact that their very name 'proved.' Any Slav who had achieved an education had, by that fact, flown in the face of his own nature."[4] Nearly three thousand Catholic priests died in Poland alone. Some of them were gunned down in their sanctuaries and in the streets; some were sent to concentration camps, where they died of starvation, disease, or torture; and some were sent to extermination camps, where they died in the infamous "shower baths" with clergy of all faiths and laity of all nationalities.

"Poles were among the first to die in the gas chambers of Auschwitz," wrote survivor M. I. Zawadzki. "More than a million Poles perished in the camps. But, unlike the Jews, most of the Poles died outside of the gas chambers. . . ."[5] Theirs was a different death: They were shot down in the streets and in the fields, they were hanged from trees, and they were worked to death in German factories and farms. In some Polish villages, SS units turned cruelty into a sick kind of sport. They would force a group of people into a wooden building, then set it on fire and listen to the screams of their dying victims. Sharpshooters waited outside to shoot down anyone who tried to escape. It was all part of Hitler's plan to reduce the population of Poles and other Slavs and to turn the survivors into slaves.

After the Nazis attacked the Soviet Union in June 1941, Ukrainians, Belorussians, and Russians were marked for the same fate as the Poles. The plight of Soviet prisoners of war was especially brutal. To the Nazis, they were not soldiers fighting for a sovereign nation—they were *untermenschen*, unworthy of being treated according to Geneva Convention rules for prisoners of war. Thousands died in concentration camps, where they were tortured, starved, or forced into labor so demanding that they died of exhaustion.

The Gypsy Purges

The name Gypsy makes most people think of colorful wagons, soulful violins, and fortune-tellers peering into crystal balls. The Gypsies are an ancient people, believed to be descended from nomadic tribes from northwest India. In the early Middle Ages, they found their way across Persia (modern Iran) and Armenia to the Balkans and Hungary. They worked as traveling handymen, mending pots and pans, as woodcarvers, horse traders, and minstrels.

Gypsies placed little value on regular working hours, permanent addresses, or political loyalties; they discouraged education for fear that it would make their children forget Gypsy ways. There was simply no place for these people in a brutal, well-ordered Nazi world, so the hierarchy ordered that they be destroyed. The process began in Germany and occupied Poland; then it spread through Europe as other countries fell under Nazi control. In areas where the Gypsy population was small, self-contained, and easy to identify, the Nazis did not bother with deportation and internment. Einsatzgruppen simply rounded up all the Gypsies and slaughtered them on the spot. According to historian Bohdan Wytwycky, "where the administrative area was small and the Gypsies were easy to identify and isolate, for example in Estonia, the annihilation of the Gypsy population is estimated to have been complete."[6]

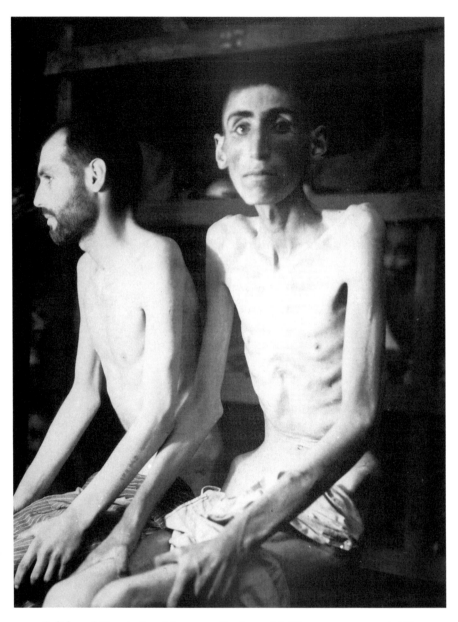

Polish and Dutch slave laborers at Buchenwald. These men averaged 160 pounds each when they entered the camp. By the time this picture was taken eleven months later, their weight had dropped to an average of only 70 pounds.

Uncle Mengele

By 1942, Gypsies who had survived the purges were being rounded up and deported to Auschwitz, arriving in such numbers that the Nazis created a special camp for them. It was in that filthy, typhus-ridden camp that SS doctor Joseph Mengele first protected, then destroyed hundreds of Gypsy children.

Mengele was a striking man with cold, dead eyes and hair sweeping back from a widow's peak. Some said he looked like an old-time movie hero; others thought he resembled Count Dracula. He could kill a human being as easily as another man might swat a fly. While even the most Nazified of the officers could become queasy about evaluating a new group of prisoners to decide who would live and who would die, Mengele thrived on the selections. When a train arrived with its human cargo, he would sit on the railway platform like the ruler of some ancient and barbarous kingdom, pointing left, right, then left again, always with perfect calm.

As chief doctor of the Gypsy camp, Mengele became fascinated by the Gypsy children. He would bring them food and candy, even take them for short outings. They called him Uncle Mengele and looked forward to his visits and to the treats he would bring.

Then came the order from SS headquarters: On August 1, 1944, the entire Gypsy camp was to be liquidated. Mengele did not hesitate to take advantage of the children's trust and affection for him. On the day of the gassings, he bustled around the camp, organizing, giving orders, attending to the smallest details. He personally drove a carload of Gypsy children to the gas chambers, talking to them all the while in the gentle, reassuring voice they had come to love.

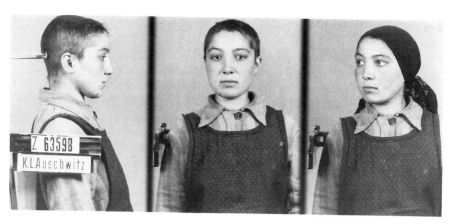

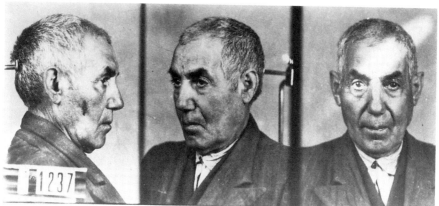

Gypsies fascinated Joseph Mengele, the man they called "Dr. Auschwitz." These individuals, shown here in their camp "mug shots," were inmates at the Gypsy camp where Mengele conducted many of his inhumane experiments.

Four thousand Gypsies died that day, and the camp was closed down. Any Gypsies who arrived afterward went straight to the gas chambers. By the time the war ended, the Nazis had killed nearly one third of the Gypsy population in Europe—a quarter of a million men, women, and children.

Genocide on Trial

When Germany surrendered on May 8, 1945, a stunned world began to realize the true horror of Nazi crimes against humanity. Allied commander General Dwight D. Eisenhower made certain that the German people knew what had happened. He ordered that thousands of civilians be required to walk through the death camps, looking at the showers that weren't showers, the crematoria that operated day and night, the piles of corpses discovered in mass graves.

At Nuremberg, where Hitler's law had stripped Jews of German citizenship, an international tribunal put twenty-two major Nazi leaders on trial for crimes against humanity. On October 1, 1946, the court sentenced twelve to hang, gave seven prison terms of various lengths, and acquitted three.

In twelve later trials, called the Nuremberg Proceedings, the court heard charges against the people who staffed the camps, ran the deportation trains, operated the gas chambers, and generally performed the workaday business of running the world's first killing bureaucracy. What had turned ordinary, basically decent human beings into the willing tools of a psychopathic regime? In a series of historic decisions, the Nuremberg judges confronted the issue of individual responsibility. They ruled against the "I was just doing my job" defense that has been the cry of the underling since King Ashurnasirpal's soldiers obeyed his orders to cut off the hands

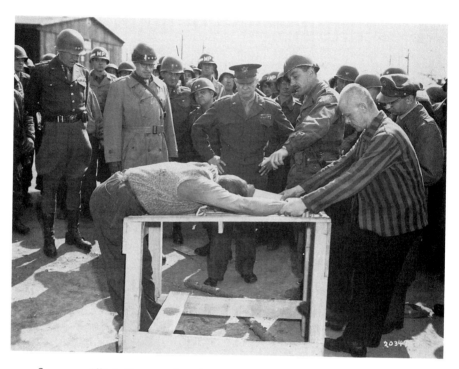

Supreme Allied Commander General Dwight D. Eisenhower watches grimly while concentration camp survivors demonstrate one of the ways they were tortured by sadistic guards and camp officials. Generals Omar Bradley and George Patton are at his right.

and feet of all captives and pile the victims up to die. The verdicts were based, not upon a person's orders, but upon whether the person knowingly and deliberately had made a moral choice.

To the dismay of the court, it was plain that, at one time or another, many of these lower-level functionaries did have a choice, and they chose to kill. That decision cost the lives of sixteen million civilians who died as a direct result of Nazi genocidal policies. That number includes Jews, Poles, Ukrainians, Russians, Belorussians, Gypsies, homosexuals, political and religious dissidents, and "undesirables" who were too old, too ill, or too handicapped to be of use in the "glorious" Third Reich.

Today, the specter of the Holocaust continues to haunt people of all races, religions, and creeds. We build monuments and museums, record survivor testimonies, teach, preach, and analyze, all to memorialize the dead and remind the living of what can happen when hatred for "the other" overcomes ethics and common decency.

8

The Killing Fields
of Cambodia

On the morning of April 17, 1975, a group of insurgents called the Khmer Rouge (Red Khmer) took the capital city of Phnom Penh, ending five long years of civil war in Cambodia. The bloody struggle pitted the China-backed Khmer Rouge against another Communist faction, backed by Vietnam, as well as the anti-Communist government of General Lon Nol. The taking of Phnom Penh in April was the culmination of an offensive begun in January.

In the conquered city, there was a great deal of confusion over what to expect from the Khmer Rouge; no one seemed to know much about them. Some called them nationalists; others said they were Communists. Still others said it didn't matter, the important thing was the result they would achieve—a new era of peace and plenty in an ancient, ravaged land. "I certainly did not believe [they] were anything but patriots, for I knew many people who supported them, and some who had joined them," wrote engineer Pin Yathay. "My father, who saw and spoke to countless refugees before moving to the city with the rest of the family in 1972, repeatedly said I was wrong. I used to tell him not to be so pessimistic. . . . Some might be communists, I said, but they were first and foremost Cambodians like us."[1]

A Strange Invasion

The Khmer Rouge entered Phnom Penh quietly, looking somewhat uncertain about exactly what they were supposed to be doing. They wore black pajamalike uniforms with checked scarves, called *kramars*, around their necks. Many were only children, twelve or thirteen years old, with faces too hardened for their years.

People watched and even cheered, not realizing that this silent parade was the beginning of a long national nightmare. According to Donald M. Seekins in *Cambodia: A Country Study*, school administrator Ith Sarin, once a member of the Khmer Rouge, "revealed the secrecy with which the Khmer Rouge concealed the existence of the communist party, which they referred to by the sinister term *Angkar Loeu* (High Organization), or simply, Angkar."[2]

At the core of *Angka* (or *Angkar*) was a small group of Paris-educated leftists under the leadership of Saloth Sar, who called himself *Pol Pot* (Original Khmer). In her history of the Cambodian revolution, journalist Elizabeth Becker comments on the meaning of this pseudonym, saying that it revealed "Saloth Sar's high degree of nationalism and his extraordinary presumption. It is an exclusive name, the name of a man who considers himself the superior leader."[3]

Pol Pot understood the power of the Big Lie, a concept that Adolf Hitler described soon after he came to power:

> The size of the lie is a definite factor in causing it to be believed . . . for the vast masses are . . . more easily deceived than they are consciously and intentionally bad. The primitive simplicity of their minds renders them a more easy prey to a big lie than a small one, for they themselves often tell little lies but would be ashamed to tell a big one.[4]

Hitler used the technique to build a propaganda machine that taught a nation how to hate and how to kill. Pol Pot used it to weave layer upon layer of secrecy around himself and Angka Loeu, until the genocide in Cambodia took on an eerie quality unlike anything the world had seen before. Like Stalin in Ukraine, Angka Loeu planned to destroy the existing peasant culture by executing its leaders and anyone else who could not adapt to a spartan, collectivized existence.

Murder and Trickery

In Phnom Penh, Khmer Rouge soldiers went from street to street and door to door, telling everyone to evacuate as quickly as possible. American B-52s were going to bomb the city, they said. As soon as the danger had passed, everyone could return to their homes. In a matter of hours, a steady stream of people trudged out of Phnom Penh. Years after that evacuation, a young woman named Teeda Butt Mam recalled it with painful clarity:

> From . . . our balcony, we noticed a trickle of residents from other districts trudging down the streets. By early afternoon, the trickle had become a flood. Rumor had it that everyone must prepare to leave the city. At once! The Angka "requested" it. . . . Herded along by the

Khmer Rouge, frightened residents streamed toward the four main thoroughfares leading to the city outskirts. . . . Those moving too slowly, turning aside to rest, or even stopping to adjust their loads were threatened by gun-wielding soldiers. With occasional shots fired overhead, the masses were kept moving.[5]

By the time people realized they were never going home, it was too late. They had followed a lie into the countryside, and now Phnom Penh lay behind them, its streets deserted. Angka had decided that cities were evil and should be abolished, along with money, mail service, telephones, schools, colleges, and libraries.

General Lon Nol, who had ruled Cambodia since he deposed Prince Norodom Sihanouk in 1970, had been forced to leave the country on April 1, 1975. Two weeks later, Phnom Penh's outer defenses fell, and the Khmer Rouge took control. They immediately sent out a message to all soldiers who fought for the ousted government: Lay down your arms and surrender, Angka said, and you will not be regarded as traitors, but welcomed as friends and countrymen.

At a hastily organized processing center in the town of Battambang, surrendering government troops were fed and treated with courtesy. As a token of good faith, the Khmer Rouge invited ranking officers to attend welcoming ceremonies for Prince Sihanouk, who was returning to Cambodia after living in exile during the Lon Nol years. More than three hundred officers put on their dress uniforms and left Battambang in a jubilant convoy, bound for the festivities in Phnom Penh.

Sergeant Major Sem Vann watched them leave. Eleven days later, Sem and the rest of the noncommissioned officers were set free to return to their home villages. Sem and thirteen other men headed toward Phnom Penh on the first leg of their homeward journey. Not far from a place called Mount Tippadei, the fifteen companions came across bodies, sprawled everywhere, all of them in dress uniforms. These were the Battambang officers. "There were hundreds of them," Sem told American journalists. "The fifteen of us . . . were revolted. All our commanding officers were lying there dead."[6]

Mount Tippadei was only one of many mass execution sites, scattered over the lush Cambodian countryside. Years after the fall of Angka Loeu, Western journalists documented dozens of these "killing fields," as the press came to call them, containing as many as sixteen thousand bodies.

Shaping the New Order

After purging the leadership, Angka began remaking society in its own image, creating a precarious existence where life was cheap and individuality forbidden. Everyone knew the ominous slogan of the Khmer Rouge: "To keep you is no benefit: To destroy you is no loss." Those words summed up life for thousands of Cambodians, and death for thousands more.

City people were taken into the deep forest, where they were forced to clear the land, build makeshift villages, and plant the fields with crops that Angka ordered them to grow. These exiles from the cities were surrounded by established settlements of *Old People*, peasants who had lived their whole lives as farmers and now resented the inept *New People*. They knew nothing about the traditional rhythms of planting and harvest. Angka exploited this rivalry to keep both groups under control.

Like Stalin in Ukraine, Angka Loeu used mass execution only for intellectuals, political leaders, military officers, and others who represented an overt threat to their rule. When those executions were finished, they killed additional tens of thousands by what the United Nations convention on genocide described as "deliberately inflicting . . . conditions of life calculated to bring about its physical destruction in whole or in part."[7]

"The greatest causes of death were hunger, disease, and exposure," wrote United States Army writer/researcher Donald M. Seekins. "Many city people could not survive the rigors of life in the countryside, the forced marches, and the hard physical labor. People died from the bites of venomous snakes, drowned in flooded areas during the rainy season, and were killed by wild beasts in jungle areas. Many fell victim to malaria."[8]

To these hazards, Angka added another: *chhoeu sattek* ("memory sickness"). While genocide survivors and human rights activists have stressed the need to preserve memory, Angka Loeu stressed the need to abolish it.

"Anyone with photos or heirlooms could be accused of memory sickness," said Teeda Butt Mam.

> A special symptom was failure to report for a full day's work. Rather than force a person to work against his will . . . a solicitous leader simply dropped by the person's hut and casually said, "Don't worry. . . . If you worry, you might think about the *old days*." The implied threat that the person might be accused of memory sickness was usually enough to get the worker back on his feet and into the fields. . . . Those with acute or chronic memory sickness were sent to see Angka.[9]

Everyone in the villages knew what that meant. Nobody ever came back from being "sent to Angka."

The Unnecessary People

In addition to killing troublesome individuals, the Khmer Rouge slaughtered whole groups of "surplus" villagers, people whose continued existence might be a drain on scarce resources. A favorite technique for gathering victims was to trick people into selecting themselves for execution. When time came to reduce population, the Khmer Rouge would order a village chief to provide lists of people who fell into specified categories: families of men who had already been reassigned, people who came from a certain city, or perhaps those who had names that sounded more Vietnamese than Cambodian.

Those on the list would be invited to resettle in pleasant new villages where they would have better housing, more generous rations, and the opportunity to build a secure and even prosperous life. With such inducements, whole families willingly signed up for relocation.

On moving day, convoys of trucks, busses, and even ox-carts arrived in each village. People scurried about, finishing their last-minute packing. No need to bother with bulky items, the soldiers told them. In the new villages, everything would be provided. With laughter, good wishes, and tearful good-byes to friends who remained behind, the settlers began their journey.

When the trucks stopped along some peaceful, tree-lined road, excited people clambered out of the trucks and scurried to keep up with the soldiers who were escorting them to their new homes. But, when they arrived at the appointed place:

> . . . they hesitated, then tried to retreat. Before them gaped newly dug trenches, an abandoned reservoir, a well, or an old mine shaft. Horrified, villagers were ordered at gunpoint to line up. Their elbows were tied

Cambodians by the thousands risked their lives to escape Khmer Rouge terror. These refugees have just arrived at Pleiku Air Force Base on one leg of their long journey to freedom.

behind their backs with red cord and they were made to kneel along the open trench. . . . Soldiers administered a quick blow to the back of the head or neck with a heavy wooden hoe or a machete. Each soldier was able to kill villagers at the rate of twenty to thirty per minute with little noise or wasted bullets.[10]

The Fall of Angka Loeu

In January 1979, Vietnamese troops captured Phnom Penh and shattered the power of Angka Loeu. Pol Pot and his Khmer Rouge loyalists fled to a stronghold near the Thai-Cambodian border, to fight a guerrilla war that has lasted into the 1990s.

In a country of seven and a half million people, between two and three million perished during Angka Loeu's reign of terror. Thousands more fled their ruined land, to settle in the United States, Canada, Australia, and other countries. Many of the refugees have become a voice for those they left behind, both the living and the dead. Like the survivors of other genocides, they bear witness for those who can no longer speak for themselves. Pin Yathay summed up the horror:

> The tragedy of Cambodia has not yet run its course, nor will it for generations. . . . Millions have died, a culture has vanished. The personal consequences of such a tragedy are incalculable, comparable only to the destruction wrought by the Black Death in Europe, by the Jewish Holocaust and by the Stalinist gulag [Soviet prison camp].[11]

9

The New Tribalism

As the twentieth century draws to a close, so does the era of superpowers, iron curtains, and arms races. Governments no longer insist that national defense requires a nuclear arsenal that can destroy the world six times over. Instead of entering an era of peace, however, we seem to be facing a new kind of war, a war of people rather than governments—an ethnic war.

In 1993, the United Nations High Commissioner for Refugees cited twenty-five ethnic conflicts that involved "the regular use of violence, including mass killings and ethnic warfare. Including older groups of displaced people, the commissioner lists 261 minority groups that have left their homelands because of political, religious, or ethnic violence in 38 countries around the world."[1]

The Culture of "Us Versus Them"

When does this violence cross the line into genocide as it is defined by the United Nations? Even the experts cannot agree, especially where contemporary events are concerned. In the 1990s, a glance at any newspaper on any given day reveals ethnic clashes in places like Bosnia, Somalia, and Rwanda. World leaders argue back and forth, trying to understand what is happening and to decide what to do about it. Amid the doubts and discussions, there is one certainty: Too many people all over the world are suffering and dying because they belong to the "wrong" racial, ethnic, or religious group.

By its very nature, ethnic warfare tends to be particularly savage; it is a war of civilians, not soldiers, fought over issues that are more emotional than political. Every human being is a potential warrior for his or her own group and therefore is a legitimate target for the enemy.

The breakdown of old political systems has left many people adrift, unsatisfied by a mechanized mass culture that belongs to nobody because it tries so hard to belong to everybody. In seeking something better and more meaningful, people are looking to their roots, to the ethnic identities and religious traditions that give them a sense of belonging and pride. By itself, this is not a bad thing; it is healthy for people to be part of something larger than themselves, an *us* that defines the boundaries of each individual life. The problem occurs when that *us* squares off against a world full of *thems*.

In an article on what some observers call "the new tribalism," journalist Robin Wright asserts her beliefs:

> Indeed, xenophobia [hatred or distrust of foreigners or strangers], religious rivalry and general intolerance of anything different are often more anguishing and cruel—not to mention costly in human lives and material

destruction—than the ideological differences that until recently divided the world.[2]

Ethnic Warfare in Bosnia

The former Yugoslavia was a patchwork nation, created after World War I from the remains of the Austro-Hungarian and Ottoman empires. Many different ethnic groups formed an uneasy alliance held together by the Communist regime of Marshal Tito (Josip Broz). When the Communist system failed, the nation fell apart as one province after another declared independence.

Bosnia's secession immediately plunged the new nation into a civil war that locked three major ethnic groups—Serbs, Croats, and Muslims—into a struggle for dominance. Bosnian Muslims are descended from Slavs who converted to Islam during the long Turkish occupation; Serbs are Eastern Orthodox Christians; Croats are Roman Catholics. Though all are Slavs, speaking different but related languages, each has been accused of committing "ethnic cleansing" against the other two.

In April 1992, Serb forces surrounded the city of Sarajevo and began shelling the civilian population. Schools and public services shut down, and a shaken population learned to conduct the business of living under constant threat of death. After five hundred days of shelling, Bosnia's health ministry reported 9,284 people killed or missing in Sarajevo and 54,398 wounded.

In the midst of this insanity, eleven-year-old Zlata Filipovic recorded in her diary, which she called Mimmy, her feelings about the hatreds dividing her world.

Thursday, November 19, 1992

Dear Mimmy,

Nothing new on the political front . . . we are dying, freezing, starving, crying, parting with our friends, leaving our loved ones. . . . Among my girlfriends, among our friends, in our family, there are Serbs and Croats and Muslims. It's a mixed group and I never knew who was a Serb, a Croat or a Muslim. . . . Now politics has started meddling around. It has put an "S" on Serbs, an "M" on Muslims and a "C" on Croats, it wants to separate them. . . . I simply don't understand it. Of course I'm "young," and politics are conducted by "grown-ups." But I think we "young" would do it better. We certainly wouldn't have chosen war.[3]

Zlata's family escaped Sarajevo just before Christmas, in 1993, but millions of others—Serbs, Croats, and Muslims—remain behind, trapped in an endless round of "ethnic cleansing" that no one seems able to stop. "What we are hoping for," said the Reverend Dobrivoje Milunovic, a Serbian priest who now lives in the United States, "is that peace will come and that it is peace that all sides can believe in. When children are dying, it doesn't matter whose they are."[4]

Clan Warfare in Somalia

On January 27, 1991, a group called the United Somali Congress toppled the government of Mohamed Siad Barre. For twenty-one years Siad had ruled the country with an iron hand, calling himself *Guulwaadde* (Victorious Leader) and building a government based upon his own blend of Marxist ideology and Muslim faith. When he was gone, that government collapsed, and Somalia fell into anarchy.

Somali society once was dominated by six clan-families, each composed of several individual clans, which were themselves composed of numerous lineages. In the post-Barre era, these clans reasserted their ancient claims and revived their ancient hatreds. Under the leadership of self-proclaimed warlords, clan fought clan, each trying to destroy the others. The genocidal conflict left thousands dead and one fourth of the population starving. The entire infrastructure of the country broke down. "There was no government, no administration, no electricity, no running water," wrote Dr. Rony Brauman, president of the humanitarian organization Doctors Without Borders.

> There were no schools, no telephones. Looters had emptied former government buildings, stripped parts from trucks and tractors, dug up electric cables for the copper in them, stolen the very pumps that brought water from the ground. The only thing Somalia had in abundance was death.[5]

The nightly news brought horrifying images of starving children, refugees, and burned buildings, and warlords locked in power struggles that threatened to wipe out an entire population. For the first time in history, United States and United Nations troops went into a country to prevent the collapse of an entire culture. They saved some lives by making sure that food and medical supplies got through to the people who needed them, but they were not able to eliminate the tribalism at the root of Somalia's national agony.

The United States experience in Somalia taught a grim lesson about military intervention: It can't solve the underlying problem. Guns can protect supplies for starving refugees, keep an uneasy peace in the streets, guard leaders while they negotiate with one another, but guns cannot change minds. That requires people of goodwill who can look beyond their "us versus them" mentality to the fundamental humanity that everyone shares.

Slaughter in Rwanda

On April 6, 1994, Rwandan president Juvenal Habyarimana died in a plane crash while trying to land in the Rwandan capital of Kigali. The cause of that crash was shrouded in mystery, but the effect was all too clear. In the following weeks, the tiny, jewellike country of Rwanda was the scene of a slaughter so terrible that even battle-hardened soldiers and seasoned war correspondents were horrified.

Within two weeks, more than one hundred thousand people had been shot or hacked to death. By May 1, the estimated death toll was two hundred thousand. Newspapers around the world showed pictures of starving, terrified refugees, and children with machete wounds in the backs of their necks. Whole towns became wastelands, with unburied corpses lying in the streets.

The two major tribes of Rwanda—Hutu and Tutsi—share the same race, religion, culture, and language. They have been a single people within a national state longer than the United States has been a nation, yet from time to time peaceful relations have been broken by outbreaks of ethnic hatred.

In 1973, the coup that brought President Habyarimana to power resulted in a brutal attack upon Tutsis by the majority Hutus. Mathilde Mukantabana, who teaches American History at Consumnes River College, near Sacramento, California, was a seventeen-year-old schoolgirl in 1973. She remembers in vivid detail the night soldiers came to her dormitory at a Catholic boarding school. They roused everyone out of bed and announced that all Tutsi students had to be out of the country before daybreak. In a desperate midnight march, Mukantabana and her schoolmates made it through the hills of western Rwanda and across the border into Zaire. Most of them never saw their families again.

After twenty years, Mukantabana still cannot understand how or why it happened. "We had all lived together ever since there were people in Rwanda," she told *Sacramento Bee* columnist Fahizah Alim. "We speak the same Bantu language, and practice the same religions and culture. Hutus and Tutsis had established a closeness and there was a lot of inter-marriage. Often you can't even tell by looking at a person what tribe he belongs to."[6]

The plane crash that killed President Habyarimana triggered old hatreds, igniting "a murderous spree by extremists from the majority Hutus against rival Tutsis and those Hutus who had opposed the government," according to Associated Press correspondent Mark Fritz.[7]

Rampaging Hutus left a trail of slaughter that included the grammar school in Gikongoro, where 88 Tutsi students were hacked to death; the town of Kibongo, where 2,800 people were massacred with grenades, knives, and submachine guns; the yellow brick church in Karubamba where Hutu soldiers violated the traditional safe haven of a religious sanctuary to execute everyone inside. Rwanda, Somalia, and Bosnia are only a few of the ethnic hot spots where massive human rights violations are ripping apart the fabric of society. They demonstrate that ethnic hatreds can gnaw at people until something triggers an explosion: a plane crash that kills a president, a coup that topples a government, a political philosophy that fails.

According to Kurt Jonassohn's "early warning system" for identifying beginning genocides, these conflicts, which involve ethnic hatreds and massive human rights violations, merit close attention from the world community of nations, human rights organizations, and people of goodwill everywhere.

10

Toward Diversity and Tolerance

During the early days of Hitler's rise to power, a German Lutheran pastor named Martin Niemöller saw the danger of Nazi racism and dared to speak out against it. He was arrested in 1938 and sent to Dachau, where he remained until the camp was liberated by Allied forces in 1945. Like other survivors, Reverend Niemöller tried to understand what had happened. How did the German people allow a small group of extremists to transform a civilized nation into a killing machine? His answer to that question has been quoted many times, by many different people.

> In Germany, the Nazis first came for the Communists, and I didn't speak up because I wasn't a communist. Then they came for the Jews and I didn't speak up because I wasn't a Jew. Then they came for the trade unionists, and I didn't speak up because I wasn't a trade unionist. Then they came for the Catholics, but I didn't speak up because I was a

A German girl is sickened as she walks past the exhumed bodies of slave workers murdered by SS guards. Before reburial, the victims were laid here so that townspeople could view the work of their Nazi leaders.

Protestant. Then they came for me, and by that time there was no one left to speak for me.

Niemöller's statement means as much in the 1990s as it did in the 1930s. There are still places where terror and mass slaughter are daily realities, where good people are silent while racism thrives. "The explosion of communal violence is the paramount issue facing the human rights movement today," said Kenneth Ross of Human Rights Watch. "And containing the abuses committed in the name of ethnic or religious groups will be our foremost challenge for years to come."[1] The question is: How do we meet that challenge? Like most questions about anything of genuine importance, this one has no easy answer.

"I Must Bear Witness"

Survivors of genocide seem to have a deep, nearly irresistible need to document and record what they have felt and experienced and suffered. In the act of bearing witness, they are paying tribute to the dead and beginning the long process of healing their own lives. They are also creating a body of testimony that will stand in spite of all efforts to forget the genocide, or pretend it never happened.

Memory, to survivors of death camps and killing fields, is a necessary thing; to those who did the killing it is a danger-ous thing, to be extinguished at all costs. "The destruction of memory is both the function and the aim of totalitarianism,"[2] wrote Czech novelist Milan Kundera, and half a world away in Pol Pot's Cambodia, Angka Loeu struggled to wipe out "memory sickness."

In the name of memory, Cambodian refugees like Pin Yathay and Teeda Butt Mam recorded their experiences,

As part of documenting Nazi savagery in World War II, a French guide shows an American officer the crematorium at Flossenburg, still full of human ashes. Toward the end of the war, these ovens burned round the clock.

General Eisenhower documented the horrors of Nazi concentration camps, and Ukranians risked their lives to keep forbidden records of the forced famine that devastated their land.

Memory took Otto Frank back to Amsterdam after World War II to find his daughter Anne's diary, and prompted the United Nations to share Zlata Filipovic's Sarajevo diary with the world. In the end, bearing witness is more than therapy for the survivors, tribute to the victims, or revenge against the killers. It is education for those who may yet learn the lessons of history—and thereby avoid repeating it.

Tolerance and Multiculturalism

By the time the killing starts, there's not much one person can do to stop it. But, there is a great deal one person can do to prevent the cycle of hatred from getting started in the first place. It requires a dedication to human rights, a willingness to speak out when they are violated, and a commitment to tolerance for different viewpoints and lifestyles.

One dictionary defines *tolerance* as freedom from bigotry and prejudice. Tolerance is not a sudden jolt of brotherly love that transforms everything it touches. It begins with little things: refusing to laugh at a racist joke, or speaking out when somebody uses derogatory labels to describe members of another racial or ethnic group.

When measured against the horrors of death camps and killing fields, tasteless humor and epithets seem trivial—but they are not. "Sticks and stones may break my bones, but words can never hurt me" is not true. It never has been.

"Negative stereotypes and the racial or ethnic slurs that are their shorthand infuse those who use them with a false sense of superiority and leaves those who are subject to them with a false sense of inferiority," wrote journalist Ronald Fitten.[3] Tolerance does not deal in stereotypes; it affirms our common humanity while respecting our differences.

At its best and most creative level, multiculturalism goes a step further and celebrates those differences. A truly multicultural society would not be a melting pot in which everybody merged into a homogenized blob called "mass culture," and it certainly would not be a battleground for mutually hostile ethnic groups. It would be a kind of cultural stew pot, with every ingredient adding to the whole yet remaining distinctly itself.

At the simplest level, multiculturalism is a rainbow coalition of humanity sharing traditions with one another. It is Cinco De Mayo in the Southwest, where everybody listens to Mariachi bands and dances together in the streets; it is gentile guests shouting "Mazel tov!" at a Jewish wedding; and it is Latinos celebrating Chinese New Year with fireworks and dragon dances.

At a deeper level, it is understanding and genuine affection for the "others" and for their ways. In such an environment people would not expect sameness, so they would not be frightened by difference. When difference became disagreement, people accustomed to a multicultural society would think of negotiation rather than extermination. Even the most devious hatemonger would have trouble spreading his poison in such a world.

In "Beyond the Melting Pot," journalist Lynell George cites a report from the Institute for the Study of Social Change:

> There would be no solution to the problems of diversity . . .
> as long as we think in polar terms. The extremes of
> "assimilation to a single dominant culture where
> differences merge and disappear vs. a situation where
> isolated and self-segregated groups retreat into . . . enclaves

At the United States Holocaust Memorial Museum in Washington, D.C., a tattered uniform from Auschwitz is mute testimony to a time and a place that humankind should never allow itself to forget.

don't work," researchers concluded. . . . The report advises a third and more viable option: "strong ethnic and racial identities (including ethnically homogenous affiliations and friendships) alongside a public participation of multiracial and multiethnic contacts that enriches the public and social sphere of life."[4]

Young people can help to build that multicultural world by learning about other cultures and sharing their own traditions in turn. They can develop friendships with people of different racial or ethnic backgrounds, become involved in the human rights movement, and learn to recognize racist propaganda when they see it. They can write letters, sign petitions, and refuse to join organizations that discriminate on the basis of race or ethnicity.

Preventing genocide is an ongoing task. Human nature being what it is, there will continue to be demagogues who crave power and fanatics who think they have a corner on the truth. There will be murderers and madmen who prey upon the innocent, and supposedly good, decent people who help them do it. Holocaust survivor and Nobel Prize-winner Elie Wiesel wrote:

> Now, on the threshold of the twenty-first century, it is our responsibility to combat the spreading cancer of fanaticism. . . . It must be constantly fought, because it leads to dehumanizing, degrading and contagious hatred. Nothing good, nothing worthy, nothing creative can be born of hatred. Hatred begets hatred. That is why we must . . . vanquish it before we even see the shadow of its shadow. How can we do this? By celebrating, cherishing, defending the liberty of others—of *all* others. At stake is our cultural, ethical and moral future.[5]

Chapter Notes

Chapter 1

1. Milton Meltzer, *Never to Forget: The Jews of the Holocaust* (New York: Dell Publishing Co., 1984), p. 68.

2. "It is a Memory of Hell," *Newsweek* (November 14, 1988), p. 42.

3. Ibid.

4. William L. Shirer, *The Rise and Fall of the Third Reich: A History of Nazi Germany* (New York: Fawcett Crest, 1962), pp. 581–582.

5. Ibid. p. 585.

Chapter 2

1. Martin Gilbert, *The Holocaust: A History of the Jews of Europe During the Second World War* (New York: Holt, Rinehart & Winston, 1985), p. 64.

2. California State Board of Education, *Model Curriculum for Human Rights and Genocide* (Sacramento: California State Department of Education, 1988), p. 2.

3. Kurt Jonassohn, "Prevention Without Prediction," *Holocaust and Genocide Studies*, vol. 7, no. 1 (New York: Oxford University Press, 1993), p. 2.

4. Ibid.

5. Ibid. p. 3.

6. Ibid. pp. 3–4.

7. "Histoire amonyme de la première croisade," ("Anonymous History of the First Crusade") ed. L. Brehier, trans.

James Bruce Ross, *The Portable Medieval Reader* (New York: Viking Press, 1949), p. 443.

8. Norman F. Cantor, *Medieval History: The Life and Death of a Civilization* (New York: Macmillan, 1969), p. 418.

9. Jonassohn, p. 5.

Chapter 3

1. California State Board of Education, *Model Curriculum for Human Rights and Genocide* (Sacramento: California State Department of Education, 1988), p. 29.

2. Ralph K. Andrist, *The Long Death: The Last Days of the Plains Indian* (New York: Collier Books, 1964), p. 8.

3. Robert V. Remini, *Andrew Jackson* (New York: Twayne Publishers, 1966), p. 129.

4. *Native American Testimony: A Chronicle of Indian-White Relations from Prophesy to the Present, 1492–1992*, ed. Peter Nabokov (New York: Viking Penguin Books, 1991), p. 151.

5. Benson J. Lossing, *Our Country: Vol. I, U.S. History on CD-ROM* (Parsippany, N.J.: Bureau Development, Inc., 1991).

6. Andrist, p. 205.

7. *The Missions of California: A Legacy of Genocide*, eds. Rupert Costo and Jeannette Henry Costo (San Francisco: American Indian Historical Society, 1987), p. 123.

8. Ibid.

9. Lynwood Carranco and Estle Beard, *Genocide and Vendetta: The Round Valley Wars of Northern California* (Norman, Okla.: University of Oklahoma Press, 1981), p. 63.

10. *Collected Documents on the Causes and Events in the Bloody Island Massacre of 1850*, ed. Robert Fleming Heizer (Berkeley: Department of Anthropology, University of California, 1973), p. 56.

11. Ibid. p. 13.

12. Ibid. p. 11.

13. Carranco and Beard, p. 94.

14. Dee Brown, *Bury My Heart at Wounded Knee* (New York: Holt, Rinehart & Winston, 1970), p. 82.

15. Andrist, p. 89.

16. Brown, p. 86.

17. Andrist, p. 155.

18. Ibid. p. 338.

19. John G. Neihardt, *Black Elk Speaks* (New York: Washington Square Press, 1972), p. 230.

Chapter 4

1. Lord Kinross, *The Ottoman Centuries: The Rise and Fall of the Turkish Empire* (New York: William Morrow & Co., 1977), p. 560.

2. Ibid. p. 574.

3. Margot Stern Strom and William S. Parsons, *Holocaust and Human Behavior* (Watertown, Mass.: International Educations, 1982), pp. 366–367.

4. Richard G. Hovannisian, *Armenia on the Road to Independence, 1918* (Berkeley: University of California Press, 1967), p. 42.

5. Strom and Parsons, p. 322.

6. Donald E. Miller and Lorna Touryan Miller, *Survivors: An Oral History of the Armenian Genocide* (Berkeley: University of California Press, 1993), p. 78.

7. Kerop Bedoukian, *Some of Us Survived: The Story of an Armenian Boy* (New York: Farrar, Straus & Giroux, 1979), pp. 19–20.

8. Ibid. pp. 21–22.

Chapter 5

1. Anton Antonov-Ovseyenko, *The Time of Stalin: Portrait of Tyranny* (New York: Harper and Row, 1981), p. 278.

2. Aleksandr I. Solzhenitsyn, *The Gulag Archipelago*, Vol. I–II (New York: Harper and Row, 1973), p. 55.

3. Ibid. pp. 56–57.

4. "Soviet Policy and the Forced Famine," *Teacher's Curriculum Guide* (Jersey City, N.J.: Ukrainian National Association, undated), p. 6.

5. James Mace, "The Man-Made Famine of 1932–1933: What Happened and Why," *The Great Famine in Ukraine: The Unknown Holocaust* (Jersey City, N.J.: Ukrainian National Association, 1988), p. 28.

6. Vasily Grossman, "The Terror-Famine in Perspective," *Stalin's Forced Famine* (Jersey City, N.J.: Ukrainian National Association, undated), p. 8.

7. Mace, p. 29.

8. Clarence Manning, *Ukraine Under the Soviets* (New York: Bookman Associates, 1953), p. 7.

9. Statement of Stephan Dubovyk, in *The Great Famine in Ukraine*, p. 70.

10. Statement of "M.D.," in *The Great Famine in Ukraine*, p. 62–63.

11. "Ethnocide of Ukrainians, in the USSR," in *The Great Famine in Ukraine*, p. 86.

12. Statement of Petro Grigorenko, in *The Great Famine in Ukraine*, p. 84.

13. California State Board of Education, *Model Curriculum for Human Rights and Genocide* (Sacramento: California State Department of Education, 1988), p. 39.

Chapter 6

1. Margot Stern Strom and William S. Parsons, *Holocaust and Human Behavior* (Watertown, Mass.: International Educations, 1982), p. 158.

2. Ibid. p. 104.

3. Martin Gilbert, *The Holocaust: A History of the Jews of Europe During the Second World War* (New York: Holt, Rinehart & Winston, 1985), p. 151.

4. Robert Jay Lifton, *The Nazi Doctors: Medical Killing and the Psychology of Genocide* (New York: Basic Books, 1986), p. 159.

5. Gilbert, p. 280.

6. Ibid. p. 284.

7. Viktor E. Frankl, *Man's Search for Meaning* (New York: Washington Square Press, 1985), pp. 30–31.

8. Anne Frank, *Anne Frank: The Diary of a Young Girl* (Garden City, N.Y.: Doubleday, 1967), pp. 278–279.

Chapter 7

1. Margot Stern Strom and William S. Parsons, *Holocaust and Human Behavior* (Watertown, Mass.: International Educations, 1982), p. 319.

2. Ibid.

3. Bohdan Wytwycky, *The Other Holocaust: Many Circles of Hell* (Washington, D.C.: The Novak Report, 1980), pp. 45–46.

4. Rev. William J. O'Malley, S.J., "The Priests of Dachau," *America Magazine* (November 14, 1987).

5. M. I. Zawadzki, Ph.D., "The Genocide of the Poles," unpublished paper (Los Angeles: Polish Millennium Library, undated), p. 6.

6. Wytwycky, p. 35.

Chapter 8

1. Pin Yathay with John Man, *Stay Alive, My Son* (New York: Free Press, 1987), p. 6.

2. Donald M. Seekins, "Cambodia: A Country Study," *Countries of the World on CD-ROM* (Parsippany, N.J.: Bureau Development, 1991).

3. Elizabeth Becker, *When the War Was Over: The Voices of Cambodia's Revolution and Its People* (New York: Simon & Schuster, 1986), p. 76.

4. George Seldes, *The Great Thoughts* (New York: Ballantine Books, 1985), p. 185.

5. Joan D. Criddle and Teeda Butt Mam, *To Destroy You Is No Loss: The Odyssey of a Cambodian Family* (New York: Atlantic Monthly Press, 1987), p. 18.

6. John Barron and Anthony Paul, *Murder of a Gentle Land* (New York: Reader's Digest Press, 1977), p. 70.

7. California State Board of Education, *Model Curriculum for Human Rights and Genocide* (Sacramento: California State Department of Education, 1988), p. 2.

8. Seekins.

9. Criddle and Mam, p. 99.

10. Ibid. pp. 145–146.

11. Yathay, pp. 237–238.

Chapter 9

1. Jim Anderson, "Ranks of Ethnic Refugees Swelling," *Sacramento Bee* (December 21, 1993).

2. Robin Wright, "The New Tribalism All Over the World," *Sacramento Bee* (June 13, 1993).

3. Zlata Filipovic, *Zlata's Diary: A Child's Life in Sarajevo* (New York: Viking Penguin Books, 1994), pp. 102–103.

4. Diana Greigo Erwin, "For Serbs, Strife in Bosnia is Centuries Old," *Sacramento Bee* (April 12, 1994).

5. "A Continent's Slow Suicide," *Reader's Digest* (May 1993), pp. 110–111.

6. Mathilde Mukantabana, "Hope Falls Victim to Ancient Hatreds," *Sacramento Bee* (April 18, 1993).

7. Mark Fritz, "Rwanda Fighting Leaves a Town Dead," *Sacramento Bee* (May 14, 1994).

Chapter 10

1. Robin Wright, "The New Tribalism All Over the World," *Sacramento Bee* (June 13, 1993).

2. William Shawcross, *The Quality of Mercy: Cambodia, Holocaust and Modern Conscience* (New York: Simon & Schuster, 1984), p. 12.

3. Ronald K. Fitten, "The Harm of Racial Slurs Buries Into the American Psyche," *Sacramento Bee* (March 28, 1993).

4. Lynell George, "Beyond the Melting Pot," *Sacramento Bee* (February 7, 1993).

5. Elie Wiesel, "When Passion Is Dangerous," *Parade Magazine* (April 19, 1992), p. 21.

Bibliography

Andrist, Ralph K. *The Long Death: The Last Days of the Plains Indian.* New York: Collier Books, 1964.

Antonov-Ovseyenko, Anton. *The Time of Stalin: Portrait of Tyranny.* New York: Harper and Row, 1981.

Barron, John, and Anthony Paul. *Murder of a Gentle Land.* New York: Reader's Digest Press, 1977.

Becker, Elizabeth. *When The War Was Over: The Voices of Cambodia's Revolution and Its People.* New York: Simon & Schuster, 1986.

Bedoukian, Kerop. *Some of Us Survived: The Story of an Armenian Boy.* New York: Farrar, Straus & Giroux, 1979.

Brown, Dee. *Bury My Heart at Wounded Knee.* New York: Holt, Rinehart & Winston, 1970.

California State Board of Education. *Model Curriculum for Human Rights and Genocide.* Sacramento: California State Department of Education, 1988.

Cantor, Norman F. *Medieval History: The Life and Death of a Civilization.* New York: Macmillian, 1969.

Carranco, Lynwood, and Estle Beard. *Genocide and Vendetta: The Round Valley Wars of Northern California.* Norman, Okla.: University of Oklahoma Press, 1981.

Costo, Rupert, and Jeannette Henry Costo, eds. *The Missions of California: A Legacy of Genocide.* San Francisco: American Indian Historical Society, 1987.

Criddle, Joan D., and Teeda Butt Mam. *To Destroy You Is No Loss: The Odyssey of a Cambodian Family.* New York: Atlantic Monthly Press, 1987.

Filipovic, Zlata. *Zlata's Diary: A Child's Life in Sarajevo.* New York: Penguin Books, 1994.

107

Frank, Anne. *Anne Frank: The Diary of a Young Girl.* Garden City, N.Y.: Doubleday, 1967.

Frankl, Viktor E. *Man's Search for Meaning.* New York: Washington Square Press, 1985.

Gilbert, Martin. *The Holocaust: A History of the Jews of Europe During the Second World War.* New York: Holt, Rinehart & Winston, 1985.

Hadzewyez, Roma, George B. Zarycky, and Marta Kolomayets, eds. *The Great Famine in Ukraine, 1932–1933: The Unknown Holocaust.* Jersey City, N.J.: Ukrainian National Association, 1988.

Heizer, Robert Fleming, ed. *Collected Documents on the Causes and Events in the Bloody Island Massacre of 1850.* Berkeley: University of California, Department of Anthropology, 1973.

Hovannisian, Richard G. *Armenia on the Road to Independence, 1918.* Berkeley: University of California Press, 1967.

Kinross, Lord. *The Ottoman Centuries: The Rise and Fall of the Turkish Empire.* New York: William Morrow & Co., 1977.

Lifton, Robert Jay. *The Nazi Doctors: Medical Killing and the Psychology of Genocide.* New York: Basic Books, 1986.

Lossing, Benson J. *Our Country, Vol. I–VI.* In *U.S. History on CD-Rom.* Parsippany, N.J.: Bureau Development, Inc., 1991.

Manning, Clarence. *Ukraine Under the Soviets.* New York: Bookman Associates, 1953.

Meltzer, Milton. *Never to Forget: The Jews of the Holocaust.* New York: Harper and Row, 1976.

Miller, Donald E., and Lorna Touryan Miller. *Survivors: An Oral History of the Armenian Genocide.* Berkeley: University of California Press, 1993.

Nabokov, Peter, ed. *Native American Testimony: A Chronicle of Indian-White Relations from Prophesy to the Present 1492–1992.* New York: Viking Penguin Books, 1991.

Niehardt, John G. *Black Elk Speaks.* New York: Washington Square Press, 1972.

Remini, Robert V. *Andrew Jackson.* New York: Twayne Publishers, 1966.

Seekins, Donald M. *Cambodia: A Country Study.* In *Countries of the World on CD-Rom.* Parsippany, N.J.: Bureau Development, 1991.

Seldes, George. *The Great Thoughts.* New York: Ballantine Books, 1985.

Shawcross, William. *The Quality of Mercy: Cambodia, Holocaust and Modern Conscience.* New York: Simon & Schuster, 1984.

Shirer, William L. *The Rise and Fall of the Third Reich: A History of Nazi Germany.* New York: Fawcett Crest, 1962.

Solzhenitsyn, Aleksandr I. *The Gulag Archipelago.* New York: Harper and Row, 1973.

Strom, Margot Stern, and William S. Parsons. *Holocaust and Human Behavior.* Watertown, Mass.: International Educations, 1982.

Wytwycky, Bohdan. *The Other Holocaust: Many Circles of Hell.* Washington, D.C.: The Novak Report, 1980.

Yathay, Pin, with John Man. *Stay Alive, My Son.* New York: Free Press, 1987.

Index